D0871973

The Human Center

The Human Center

Moral Agency in the Social World

HOWARD L. HARROD

FORTRESS PRESS   Philadelphia

Library of Congress Cataloging in Publication Data

Harrod, Howard L., 1932–
   The human center

   Includes index.
   1. Ethics. 2. Social ethics. 3. Values. I. Title.
  II. Title: Moral agency in the social world.
    BJ1012.H324   170   80-2392
    ISBN 0-8006-0657-4   AACR2

8582A81   Printed in the United States of America 1-657

For Annemarie

Contents

Preface

ORDINARY MORAL EXPERIENCE often goes unnoticed and unanalyzed, and yet it exhibits some of the most marvelous instances of human transcendence. One fascination motivating this work is precisely the luminosity of the small, the common, and the mundane. In even the most banal situations, human beings remain creatures marked by symbolic imagination, loyalties, religious awareness, and a sense of beauty. These qualities may be dulled, sated, or perverted, but even in this latter state human beings do not cease to be creatures possessing capacities for transcendence. The fundamental purpose of this work is to explore some of the foundations upon which capacities such as memory, imagination, and anticipation rest and to focus attention upon the contribution of these elements to an understanding of moral experience in its mundane forms.

Reflection upon the themes expressed in this book has proceeded over time and in various contexts, gathering a number of debts which require acknowledgment. My teachers, H. Richard Niebuhr and James M. Gustafson, stand in the background and provide a sense of direction concerning what fundamental issues invite further exploration. As they certainly did, I have in my own way hewed my own line. I am grateful to them for providing such fitting examples. An early version of the argument was formulated in 1976 at Newport Beach, California. Two colleagues at the University of Southern California, John Orr and Donald Miller, were supportive of this initial effort and read subsequent drafts of the manuscript. Thanks are due as well to two groups at Vanderbilt who responded critically to portions of the argument: the Seminar in Religion in Society, taught in the spring of 1977, and the Bible and Ethics faculty group. Certain individual colleagues at Vanderbilt have been of special importance: Edward Farley, Linda Holler, Mary Kelly, Douglas Knight, Thomas Ogletree, and Peter Paris. John Reiman assisted with proofreading and prepared the index. For their contributions, both personal and professional, I am deeply grateful. At the institutional level, I should like to thank the editors of the *Journal of the American Academy of Religion* and the *Journal of Religious Ethics* for the opportunity to present earlier versions of some of these themes. And, finally, grants from the Vanderbilt University Research Council enabled me to have the leisure to imagine and to write.

Vanderbilt University   HOWARD L. HARROD

Introduction

THE CHAPTERS THAT FOLLOW are organized around the theme of the moral agent in the social world. From one perspective, they are excursions into constructive ethical reflection, a circumstance that requires further elaboration. If we understand ethics to refer generally to disciplined reflection upon the moral life in both its individual and its social manifestations, then it is clear that only a single element within a much more complex horizon has been addressed. Does not ethics also have to do with advocating what is believed to be good, right, just, or fitting? Despite the fact that each of these value terms refers to distinct historical traditions, they all point to a normative function which ethics is commonly assumed to perform. The following essays are not directly concerned with recommending norms or concrete courses of action, even though these matters are viewed as a legitimate part of the task of ethics. Rather than recommending or defending norms, the concern is to explore some of the foundations upon which moral experience and action rest.[1]

Two principal concerns govern how the argument is developed, and if these concerns are understood initially, then some confusion may be avoided later. The first concern affecting the entire analysis is the sense of pluralism that characterizes modern life. We have heard it said, perhaps *ad nauseam,* that

---

1. This view of ethics embodies the distinction between morals as a practical enterprise, concerned with recommending norms, and ethics as a reflective enterprise, concerned with the foundations of moral life and action. For a version of this distinction, see James M. Gustafson, *Christian Ethics and the Community* (Philadelphia: Pilgrim Press, 1971), p. 85.

the experience of modern people, especially those who represent urban-industrial societies, is fragmented and marked by movement among many small life-worlds.[2] Certainly this generalization applies to moral experience. There are few value paradigms that are widely shared and few norms about which there is broad social consensus. As a consequence, many individuals have retreated to the privacy of their personal experience or to the intimacy of small groups, seeking through these means to legitimate their value persuasions and actions. Such a massive retreat from public ethics has been particularly damaging to policy discussions which attempt to shape attitudes toward and evaluations of major social norms.[3]

Though motivated in part by a sense of the pluralism of modern culture and consciousness, the argument developed here will not seek to propose a new consensus, a reality which certainly will not emerge as a consequence of writing a single book! Rather, the argument is relatively modest in its beginning point, which is to explore some of the grounds upon which moral experience rests. These claims increase in significance, of course, at the point where it becomes clear that the formal conditions that constitute the moral life are held to be widely shared, if not universal in their scope. Again, it is not the content of moral experience that will be the primary focus; that content is marked by the pluralism referred to above. Rather, it is in the nature of the human being and the social world that continuities emerge which it is the task of these reflections to illuminate. Such description will reveal that moral experience is grounded in some of the same features that render other sorts of experience possible, such as aesthetic or religious awareness. It will be the further task of the argument to show, at least in a preliminary fashion, how these various experiential regions are related to one another and to their common ground.

2. An interesting treatment of this issue is by Benita Luckmann, "The Small Life-Worlds of Modern Man," *Social Research* 37, 4 (1970): 580–96.
3. Understood in one way, political discourse depends upon a certain minimal consensus. When this is not present, the public discussion concerning major social issues becomes a matter of response to pressure groups or attempts by an administrative elite to manipulate opinion. In my view, these tendencies are exhibited in contemporary discussions of energy and defense.

At this point a second major concern which lies behind the analysis may be brought into view. Generally speaking, this concern is with the effect of science and scientific paradigms upon the interpretation of vast regions of modern experience. The particular effect of interest here is the tendency toward objectification and an accompanying suspicion of subjective experience. Feelings, imaginings, fantasy, dreams, and so on are viewed as peculiarly "soft" data; and yet these are some of the phenomena that stand at the center of what we are calling moral experience. There is the temptation, which is presently very widespread, to ground these elements in "harder" facts which derive from viewing reality under the aspect of one or more scientific paradigms. There is the tendency, for example, to reduce mental phenomena to the results of chemical firing of brain synapses, following the findings of brain physiology. Or, in the social sciences, there is the persistent view that the meaning of human behavior may be reduced either to its various functions or to its conformity to mathematical models. In either case, the question of the *subjective meaning* of behavior is seriously compromised.[4]

The consequences these tendencies have for moral experience become clear when we reflect upon the fact that memory, imagination, feelings, and so on seem to be integrally involved in moral life and action. If these elements are evacuated of significance or reduced to other realities, then the moral life will tend to become an epiphenomenal rather than an essential aspect of human existence. One of the purposes of this analysis is to establish the various elements of human experience which compose moral life upon grounds that have their own relative autonomy and may not be reduced without remainder to a particular scientific paradigm.

To some, the analysis may still appear to be a reduction of

---

4. It is true, of course, that there is also resistance to and reaction against tendencies toward objectification. Despite this fact, there are still powerful forces, professionally institutionalized, which maintain interpretations of human reality that tend to evacuate the subjective and elevate the objective. These tendencies appear in various forms of behaviorism and also within many contexts of biomedical research and practice, for example.

moral experience to social or psychological realities, and thus open to the criticisms leveled above. Such an interpretation is unwarranted, however, if it is clearly understood that the intention is to establish the subjective and intersubjective foundations of moral experience upon grounds which are the conditions of possibility for the creation of scientific paradigms. For example, the paradigms of the social sciences that deal with human experience are understood as abstractions from the rich foundations of that experience. They can illuminate human experience in various important ways, but they cannot exhaust its significance. In other words, the creation of a scientific paradigm is an act of the imagination that presupposes but does not explain the act which grounds its possibility.

At this juncture, a word about method will assist in understanding the sources from which the argument derives its conceptual orientation. It will be obvious to many readers that the argument manifests long-standing interests in religious ethics and that by training and profession these interests have been shaped by a particular religious tradition, Western Christianity. Also evident are interests in the social foundations of moral and religious experience in whatever form or tradition they appear. Here the classical tradition of the sociology of religion, especially the work of Max Weber and Émile Durkheim, has made its mark. The difference between the present argument and the conceptual orientation of the classical sources of religious ethics and the sociology of religion lies in the appropriation of the phenomenological perspective, especially as it appears in the work of Alfred Schutz.[5]

5. The Schutz corpus which informs the investigation includes the following major works: Alfred Schutz, *Collected Papers*. Vol. I, *The Problem of Social Reality*, ed. Maurice Natanson (The Hague: Martinus Nijhoff, 1967); *Collected Papers*. Vol. II, *Studies in Social Theory*, ed. Arvid Brodersen (The Hague: Martinus Nijhoff, 1964); *Collected Papers*. Vol. III, *Studies in Phenomenological Philosophy*, ed. I. Schutz (The Hague: Martinus Nijhoff, 1966). Hereafter the *Collected Papers* will be cited as CP, with the appropriate volume indicated. Other works include Alfred Schutz, *The Phenomenology of the Social World*, trans. George Walsh and Frederick Lehnert (Evanston, Ill.: Northwestern University Press, 1967), hereafter cited as PSW; Alfred Schutz, *Reflections on the Problem of Relevance*, ed. Richard Zaner (New Haven, Conn.: Yale University Press, 1970), hereafter cited as PR; Alfred Schutz and Thomas Luckmann, *The Structures of the Life-World* (Evanston, Ill.: Northwestern University Press, 1973), hereafter cited as SLW.

Two comments, one about the phenomenological perspective and the other about the work of Schutz, are in order at this point. First, about the phenomenological perspective, it will become clear in the following argument that phenomenology is employed as a mode of reflection which breaks through traditional dualisms of inner/outer, self/world, self/other, immanence/transcendence, and so on. It is a view that understands the self as a center of meaning stretched out upon a world which is constituted by its own activity but which, dialectically, constitutes the possibility of its activity. Thus understood, the term "world" refers to configurations of meaning that are intersubjectively created and maintained. Moral agency will be understood as the way in which the world is apprehended in terms of a realm of value meanings. Given this perspective, the task of the analysis becomes the description of value meanings and the disclosure of their structural ground in agency and the social world. The phenomenological perspective clearly cannot provide us with moral experience; that is its limit. But such a perspective can illuminate the structures upon which moral experience is grounded; that is its possibility.[6]

Second, about the work of Schutz, it is clear that his writings were aimed at providing adequate methodological and epistemological foundations for the social sciences. One of his major contributions was to expose the taken-for-granted life world as the proper object of social science research. It is from this world that the human sciences take their departure, and it is finally to this world that they must refer their explanations, interpretations, and predictions. Schutz believed that in order for the social sciences to do their proper work, they must develop an adequate view of the phenomenon of meaning and of the human center which constituted that meaning.[7]

6. In addition to the Schutz literature, the following works have been influential in shaping the perspective of these essays: Maurice Natanson, *Edmund Husserl: Philosopher of Infinite Tasks* (Evanston, Ill.: Northwestern University Press, 1973); Maurice Natanson, *The Journeying Self* (Reading, Mass.: Addison-Wesley, 1970); Herbert Spiegelberg, *The Phenomenological Movement,* 2 vols. (The Hague: Martinus Nijhoff, 1969); Peter Berger and Thomas Luckmann, *The Social Construction of Reality* (New York: Doubleday, 1966); and Aron Gurwitsch, *The Field of Consciousness* (Pittsburgh: Duquesne University Press, 1964).

7. These views appear with great clarity in Schutz, PSW.

In elaborating his views, Schutz developed a theory of action and choice, a vision of internal time consciousness, an understanding of multiple levels of experience, and a theory of types and symbols. The present analysis employs these Schutzean themes as touchstones for constructive ethical reflection, developing them in many cases in novel directions. In a curious way, however, the starting point for these reflections is similar to that of Schutz, namely, that the problem with much contemporary ethical reflection is that it lacks an adequate view of the human being who deliberates, evaluates, chooses, and acts. It is the intention of this analysis to provide at least some elements of a consistent and comprehensive view of human moral experience. To employ other language, the argument seeks to develop some features of a philosophical anthropology which are adequate to constructive ethical reflection.[8]

Allusions to religion and to the relationship between morality, religion, and other human experiences, such as the aesthetic, appear throughout the essays that follow. But religion and religious ethics are not thematized and made the object of systematic analysis. The reason for this lies partly in the belief that an instrument of analysis can be developed which deals with the meaning structure of moral traditions without reducing these traditions to their relationship with religious beliefs.[9] In other words, the attempt is to develop a method that can penetrate moral traditions and interpret them "from within."[10] If this purpose is at least partially achieved, then it should be clear that the meaning structure of religion is often closely associated

---

8. A constructive appropriation of Schutz's views which follows his critique of the social sciences more closely than the present analysis is by Gibson Winter in his *Elements for a Social Ethic* (New York: Macmillan Company, 1966).

9. This beginning point is consistent with that assumed by H. Richard Niebuhr in *The Responsible Self* (New York: Harper & Row, 1963), pp. 45–46, and with that of James M. Gustafson in *Can Ethics Be Christian?* (Chicago: University of Chicago Press, 1975).

10. This attempt follows lines similar to those proposed by Peter Berger for the study of religious meanings. Berger suggested that Schutz could become the touchstone for the development of a theory of religion which is more adequate than that proposed by functional definitions. See "Some Second Thoughts on Substantive versus Functional Definitions of Religion," *Journal for the Scientific Study of Religion* 13(1974): 125–33.

with moral traditions, especially as they are embodied in specific cultures. If the development of the instrument of analysis is successful, then the next step would be an exploration of determinate moral and religious traditions in order to grasp their peculiar meaning structure and to assess the effect this has upon human knowing and doing. Clearly the present analysis is a prolegomenon to this more extensive and complex task.

The argument unfolds in terms of six interrelated excursions which turn back upon each other and, hopefully, advance at the same time. The task of the first chapter is to develop a theory of agency that discloses elements or "powers" of the self which must be presupposed in any account of the self as moral agent. In this chapter it becomes clear that, whatever we mean by moral agency, we must not draw a radical distinction between this phase or resolution of the self's capacities and other types of experience. Moral agency is a species of agency, generally conceived, and it depends for its existence upon conditions of possibility which give rise to multiple dimensions of experience, including the moral.

The second chapter opens with an account of how human beings appear to be "migratory" creatures who experience multiple levels of reality.[11] One of these levels is identified as the experience of value, which occurs as a consequence of entering into a province of value meanings. A central concern of the chapter is to develop a view of values as distinguishable sorts of meaning structures, on the one hand, and to give an account of the reality sense which sets them off from other sorts of experience, on the other.

The third chapter takes up the problem of how particular moral traditions may affect human knowing and acting in quite concrete ways. Here, the argument develops in terms of an analysis of five typical moral traditions: the ethics of ends, the ethics of duty, the ethics of responsibility, the ethics of consequences, and the ethics of virtue. The attempt will be to show how each of these moral traditions is actually a finite province

---

11. The language of migration is Niebuhr's. See "Towards a New Other-World-liness," *Theology Today* 1, 1 (1944): 78, 81.

of value meaning which possesses its own peculiar characteristics. Granting any one of them the accent of reality, which means entering into its meaning structure, shapes our sense of moral experience in specific ways.

The fourth chapter addresses the important and complex problem of the nature of the social world, and particularly the dimensions of that world which bear directly on the nature of moral agency. The central question of this chapter is how moral traditions arise as intersubjective realities and how they are maintained over time. In other words, the search is for social correlates of the individual experience of value. These turn out to be shared paradigms of value meaning that are maintained by certain identifiable social processes.

The fifth chapter takes up the problems of deliberation and choice. Moral action is viewed as involving the interpretation and shaping of experience in the light of a reality sense emerging from a particular province of value meanings. In order to highlight this process, the elements of deliberation and choice are viewed within the context of a crisis which renders routine moral experience problematic. It will become clear, however, that both routine and problematic contexts involve continual processes of interpretation, projection, and choice.

The final chapter takes up the question of moral communities and moral discourse. The intention of this chapter is to show how moral communities embody paradigms of value meaning, rehearse them in various sorts of ritual processes, and bring them to bear upon the taken-for-granted social world, especially if that world has become problematic. Important in this regard is a view of types and symbols as constitutive of the social world. Moral discourse comes to be understood as that process through which dimensions of value meaning that are symbolically apprehended are normatively brought to bear upon sectors of the social world.

To summarize, the goals of the argument are to build up an account of ordinary moral experience and the conditions of its possibility; to view the unity and continuity of the moral life in terms of these constitutive conditions; to portray both the persistence and fragility of moral experience in its individual and intersubjective forms; to give an account of moral experience which acknowledges both pluralism and the deep reality sense that attends particular moral traditions; and to show how the moral life is interpenetrated by experiences of aesthetic and religious meaning.

I

The Self as Agent

THE FUNDAMENTAL MEANINGS clustering around the notion of agency have to do with the power to initiate action. Within the general parameters of the root metaphor of agency, other possible human experiences may be envisioned. For example, the power to act expresses itself daily in myriad forms of human striving, from practical manipulations to the most sophisticated scientific reflections. Or, again, the power to act expresses itself in works of artistic imagination or religious contemplation. Whatever the forms of human experience, the continuity underlying all of them is the self as agent, the luminous center which stands behind and empowers all of our concrete experiences.

The initial intention of these reflections is to trace out certain elements that shed light upon the self as agent. As the description unfolds, it will build toward an image of agency which illuminates many regions of human experience. The more specific purpose for undertaking this description is to give an account, in later chapters, of experiences of value, moral experience, and actions that proceed from these grounds. The search will be for a constructive view of the human being which comes to rest in an understanding of the self as a moral agent in the social world.

Beginning an analysis which aims at grasping moral experience at such a high level of generality is motivated by the view that moral experience is a specific qualification of general human experience. Thus the foundations of moral experience and an understanding of the self as moral agent come into view, according to this analysis, only as we attend to elements that are ingredients in a more general notion of agency. The account which follows will proceed according to this method, attempting to develop an instrument of analysis which enables us to grasp the moral life and moral experience at additional depths.[1]

An example may assist the initial effort. Imagine yourself involved in a practical project, such as repairing and refinishing a piece of furniture. Any phase of your activity, from sanding the wood to repairing broken parts to applying a new finish, requires that you exercise physical effort upon an object that offers resistance. Your effort is not unfocused or generalized but is made quite specific through the application of particular skills which you have acquired from previous experience. This means that you know how to sand wood effectively, with smooth strokes and appropriate pressure, that you know the general reaction of certain finishes in relation to different kinds and qualities of wood, and that you understand the principles which relate to the repair of defective or broken parts.

There is an additional dimension that shapes your activity. Not only do you apply specific elements of previously acquired knowledge and learned skills to the project, but you also imagine a picture of the finished product. This envisioning of the outcome of embodied effort, knowledge, and skill is a powerful factor which gives additional form and purpose to your activity. And when your task is finished, the recollection of how you envisioned the outcome is a measure of whether the initial image has been adequately reflected in material form.

Imagine further that the piece of furniture upon which you work is a family heirloom. This fact may open the way for other dimensions of experience which cluster about the project and fringe it with additional horizons of meaning. These horizons may be populated by memories of others who, in another time

1. Although this account of moral agency in the social world owes an immediate debt to the phenomenological tradition, the more long-standing concerns which motivate these reflections were initially stimulated by H. Richard Niebuhr. Even though I do not exhibit concern for religious ethics generally or Christian ethics specifically, I am interested in developing a view of moral agency that will illuminate the relationship between religious experience and moral life. I approach the border of these concerns in these essays, but I do not take up the problem directly. I consider the present work as a prolegomenon to the study of religious horizons of meaning and their import for moral experience. Methodologically, I still find Niebuhr's starting point congenial and wish to affirm it as my own. See H. Richard Niebuhr, *The Responsible Self* (New York: Harper & Row, 1963), pp. 45–46.

and place, used the piece of furniture. Working upon this particular material object may evoke echoes which suffuse present experience with memories that ebb and flow while you continue to shape the object in the light of a projected vision. In such moments experience becomes dense and textured as the practical project is surrounded by meanings deriving from the depths of personal history. As your action proceeds, these meanings may be carried into each present moment, and you may be aware that they are important for the motivation of your activity; or they may rise up powerfully and unexpectedly in images charged with memorial affectivity.

Suppose also that an additional theme motivating your activity involves your intention of giving the finished piece of furniture to a son or daughter. This project may actually come to govern what becomes a subordinate activity of repairing and refinishing the piece of furniture. This larger project also includes its own subthemes, such as your desire to influence the responses of a son or daughter in such a way that he or she will come to share in the meaning of the important ancestor who once used the piece of furniture. What for others may be only an artifact, for you is an object infused with meanings to be preserved and shared.

Additional horizons may be present and may, from time to time, rise up in your experience. You may become aware, for example, of a sense of beauty and form associated with the experience of the object upon which you are working. This sensibility may be associated further with vague, generalized feelings about the importance of preserving the past and establishing continuity among the generations. In a strange way you sense that it is appropriate that the form and beauty of the object come to represent for you the continuity of kinship relationships.

In actual experience these horizons of meaning are interpenetrating, and the various projects which give them expression are not always at the center of attention. For example, if a problem emerges with the application of a finish, then this theme becomes a primary project which may occupy your energy in such a way that the image piece-of-furniture-as-gift will fade into the background of your awareness. If the practical difficulty is solved, then your experience may again be modulated by other meaning horizons which have been described. Indeed, you may make a self-conscious decision to interpret your action primarily in the light of one particular horizon, ordering other possible meaning contexts in relation to one which has become primary.

This example portrays important aspects of human agency which must now be systematically analyzed. The action described is a mundane possibility, highly familiar in form, proceeding from grounds which are taken for granted in experience. It is these prereflective and routinized elements of experience which must be subjected to further analysis. As we sort through the complexities of the example, what will emerge is a view of how experience occurs, how it is time-full, how it is embodied, and how it is essentially social. These elements will become touchstones for understanding how the self apprehends values, has moral experience, and acts as a moral agent in the social world.

HUMAN EXPERIENCE

If we reflect further upon the previous example, it becomes clear that experiencing the piece of furniture as a material object, the memories that became associated with it, and the various purposes that motivated action in relation to it can all be objects of conscious attention, but we are not necessarily conscious of them simultaneously. As was pointed out, they wax and wane as objects of conscious awareness. Such a perspective leads to the view that human conscious experience is always experience *of* something. There is no such thing as pure, contentless conscious experience; the subject who knows and the object known are in an intimate relationship with each other.

There is a mutual correlation between the object of any experience and the experiencing person's awareness. There is no way of moving below this dialectic between subject and object, to arrive at a level where consciousness is present to itself without objects. At the most primordial level, the self is still

14

present to itself as object. That the subject and object appear as pregiven is a consequence of the structure of consciousness and neither a later development nor an addition. The pairing of the self's spontaneity with objects is simply an expression of the essential structure which characterizes human consciousness wherever it appears.[2]

An important distinction may be drawn at this point. There is a difference between talking about the acts which make possible the appearance of objects of awareness and the characteristics of the objects themselves.[3] For example, we can focus attention upon the acts of recollection or upon the concrete memory of a previously experienced object, person, or event. Or we can focus attention upon the acts of perception by which we grasp the object, piece of furniture, rather than dwell upon its shape, size, color, and so on. Acts of recollection which make my memorial experience possible, acts of imagination which make my fantasy life possible, and acts of perception which etch out a world of material objects and others are distinguishable but not separable from the objects of memory, fantasy, or perception. The content of mundane experience is filled with apprehended objects of our conscious lives, whereas the structures that make such experiences possible remain largely taken for granted.

If we focus attention upon that which is routinized and taken for granted, then the initial example receives further clarification. The object, piece of furniture, appears in experience not only as a consequence of the directional grasp of consciousness; its appearance is also dependent upon a capacity to generalize or typify experience. Objects of this sort are apprehended as pieces

2. This view of how experience occurs is influenced by the theory of intentionality developed within the phenomenological tradition. The central insights I wish to appropriate here have to do with the co-constitutive relationship between subject and object within the epistemological context, and the emphasis upon consciousness as a source of meaning. See Alfred Schutz, CP, Vol. I, p. 103; Maurice Natanson, *Edmund Husserl: Philosopher of Infinite Tasks* (Evanston, Ill.: Northwestern University Press, 1973), ch. 5; and Marvin Farber, *The Foundation of Phenomenology* (Albany: State University of New York, 1968), ch. XII.
3. This point embodies a version of the distinction within the phenomenological tradition between *noesis* (acts of consciousness) and *noema* (objects of consciousness). See Schutz, CP, Vol. I, pp. 106-9; cf. Edmund Husserl, *Ideas,* trans. W. R. Boyce Gibson (New York: Collier Books, 1962), chs. 9-10.

of furniture and not trees, animals, objects of fantasy (except in our imagined projects), or persons. The fact that we do not generally confuse the objects of our experience depends upon the fact that we have learned, most primordially through language, how to identify objects in terms of their general characteristics. The capacity to typify is given; the content of a type is filled in most basically by language, which mediates the accumulated social experience of predecessors.[4]

The capacity to typify is one of the elements which makes possible our experience of a world. Not only are objects of perception apprehended typically but all other objects as well. The world is presented to us as an elaborate structure of types and is shared by all who are coextensive with our linguistic community.[5] In terms of the example, the piece of furniture is apprehended typically by us and, we presume, by all others who share our typifications. We anticipate no problem of recognition or misunderstanding at the level of meaning when we present the finished piece to a son or daughter. It will be recognized for what it is and its function will readily be understood. It is true that it may not be apprehended in terms of the intention to enhance generational identity and continuity. In order to accomplish this end, we may have to communicate the story of the object to those who receive it. By contrast, if we presented the object to a member of the Maori tribe in New Zealand, then there might be disturbances at the levels of both recognition and meaning.

This analysis of typification will be connected finally with certain human experiences of transcendence and will also be made central to the activity of interpretation, both of which bear directly upon moral experience. At this point we must continue with an analysis which is not obviously concerned with the

4. The basic view of types and typification presented here and elsewhere in these essays is influenced by the analysis of Schutz, although I do not follow him in every detail. See, for example, Schutz, CP, Vol. I, pp. 74–76; CP, Vol. II, pp. 232 ff.; SLW, pp. 233–35. The sensitive reader will also see the influence of Max Weber at many points. The general insight I am pursuing in this context is the view which holds that human beings are able to generalize their experience and that such a capacity enables them to transcend experience in various ways.

5. This analysis will be extended further in Chapter IV.

moral life in order to draw out other general conditions of human experience.

The typical perception of the object in our example as a piece of furniture is accompanied by a dimension of depth which, though experientially present, is deeply taken for granted. For instance, we do not perceive the object in question in terms of its surface only; rather, we experience the object, piece of furniture, as a unity, front side and back side. We do not consciously infer from the perception of the front side of the object that it has a back side; rather, both sides are presented simultaneously in experience. This structural feature of our conscious lives clearly adds a dimension of depth to human perception. As we move closer to actual objects of perception, it is true that our expectations about the characteristics of particular objects may be mistaken. The piece of furniture in the example is prereflectively grasped as an object with depth, front side and back side. But my concrete expectation that it has a back side composed of the same sort of wood as the front side may be mistaken. I may discover, to my disappointment, that rather than cherry, the back is actually plywood.

More important for this analysis is the way in which this object of perception became paired with other orders of experience, such as memories.[6] The ebb and flow of memorial experiences referred to earlier occur because the object in perception "wakens" memories of a particular predecessor. The specific content of the memorial experience is dependent, of course, upon previous lived experience with the predecessor. But that this meaning horizon can become paired with a particular object in my field of perception is an expression of operations of our conscious lives which are deeply routinized and taken for granted. The fact that one level of meaning can

6. The views presented here are dependent upon Schutz's analysis of the pairing capacity of human consciousness which, in turn, is an appropriation of Husserl's notion of appresentation. See Schutz, CP, Vol. I, pp. 294–97; cf. Edmund Husserl, *Cartesian Meditations,* trans. Dorion Cairns (The Hague: Martinus Nijhoff, 1973), pp. 89 ff. For an illuminating exposition and appropriation of the notion of appresentation, see Edward Farley, *Ecclesial Man* (Philadelphia: Fortress Press, 1975), pp. 197–203, 215 ff.

waken other levels of meaning provides a clue to understanding the textured richness of human experience. The horizons that are evoked in memory may, in the case of the example, vary in complexity and intensity; and they may be different memorial phases, although of the same predecessor, as we return again and again to the project of refinishing the piece of furniture. But no matter how complex or intense, these horizons are called forth in experience by the pairing capacity of human consciousness.

This pairing capacity underlies the understanding of symbol which will inform the entire analysis to follow. A preliminary definition of symbol will form the context for further elaboration. In the example we have been using, it is clear that the way piece-of-furniture-to-be-refinished is initially grasped is as an object in the field of perception with dimensions of depth which have already been indicated. As an item of perception, interpreted as a piece of furniture, and grasped in its unity, this object appears as a part of the everyday world of objects, events, and others. Notice, however, the complex structure of associations which clustered about this object of perception. It is associated with the typical grasp of other contemporaries, the son or daughter, for whom the project is intended. It may also be associated with other persons, also contemporaries, such as the individual with whom we consult concerning a finish, and so on. All associations of this type depend upon meaning structures within an everyday world which is spatially and temporally shared with others. These others may be close at hand or they may be typified by us if they are absent. In either case, they are others who are related to us as contemporaries.

But the project was also associated with predecessors, ancestors who are no longer a part of our present world, and with successors, those we expect to follow us. Furthermore, the project was associated with the intention of preserving continuity among the generations. This horizon of meaning, if subjected to further analysis, would turn out to be a sphere of value meanings, either held individually or shared with others in the social world. Finally, the experience of the object was related to an aesthetic horizon of meaning, a horizon which filled experience with a feeling of form and order, both at the level of the object itself and in terms of its function as that which establishes continuity among the generations; bordering upon this level of significance is the apprehension of the beauty and order of generational continuity.

These complex associations, with their multiple horizons, arise as a consequence of the operation of symbols. For purposes of this preliminary discussion, a symbol will be understood as an object, person, or event which stands in experience as an item of the everyday world but which becomes paired with meanings that transcend the everyday world. Symbols are conditions of possibility for migrations of experience between a sense of the everyday world and transcendent horizons of meaning.[7]

The relationship between typifying and symbolic consciousness must also be clarified. If the son or daughter for whose sake the project of refinishing the piece of furniture is being done is absent, then that person will appear in experience in typical form through memory or anticipation. Such experiences by which we grasp an absent other through types that have been built up through past associations are made possible by acts of memory and imagination. In these cases the person typified is a contemporary, a center of meaning and affectivity potentially available to our experience in a way that ancestors and successors are not. Yet in these cases experience may also be filled in with typical interpretations of predecessors and imaginal projections concerning successors. What, then, is the difference between typification and symbolic meanings, since both involve transcendence of the everyday world and both are grounded in the pairing capacity of consciousness?

In the case of typified meaning structures, we are dealing with the level of referential meaning. That is, the interpretation of the son or daughter, and even the view we have of specific

---

7. This definition of symbol is an adaptation of that which was proposed by Schutz, CP, Vol. I, p. 331. The pairing capacity of human consciousness (appresentation) underlies both typifying and symbolizing. This understanding of types and symbols will be elaborated and filled in as the argument develops.

ancestors, is built on the basis of knowledge about their specific identity. The son or daughter has a name and biography in which we have shared; and the ancestors had a context and identities which, though we may not have experienced as their contemporaries, we interpret on the basis of meanings received from others who were their contemporaries. Levels of symbolic meaning arise at the point where objects, such as the piece of furniture, or others, such as contemporaries or ancestors, become paired with horizons of meaning that transcend referential significance. We are in the presence of symbolic meaning when objects, events, and others mediate to experience a sense of beauty and form, a sense of the value of continuity among the generations, or, in the case of successors, others who we imagine will at some future time hold us as objects of both referential and symbolic significance.

There are further complications in this understanding which may be mentioned. For instance, the memory of a significant predecessor may waken the further memory of still another predecessor, and so on. The object of experience which wakens other orders of meaning may not be an item of perception at all. Fantasies, dreams, and ideal objects may, for example, waken other dimensions of our experience which rise up and occupy the stage of immediate attention. In the light of this point, the initial definition of symbol must be broadened. Objects of experience which are not a part of the everyday world may perform a symbolic function, and there may even be symbols which become paired with other symbols. Here we approach the analysis of the multivalent character of symbols, a theme we will attend to further at a later point.

The richness and complexity of this aspect of our conscious lives could be elaborated almost endlessly, but that is not our purpose. The intention of this analysis has been to prepare the way for understanding how moral experience occurs. If the argument is correct that moral experience arises upon grounds which make experience generally possible, then the analysis has exposed elements of agency that are essential to such understanding. We have shown how it is possible for objects of experience to arise and to become related to other objects; these same foundations are required for the emergence of horizons of value meaning as objects of experience. These matters will become clearer as the argument develops, and what is necessary at this point is to fill in an understanding of temporality which is illustrated by the initial example.

TEMPORALITY

The capacity to be filled with a sense of the past, to grasp present experience, and to envision a future state of affairs marks off the human being from other life forms. Sentient life forms are myriad, but the human being is distinguished by consciousness of internal time. The concrete richness and unique texture of memory and imagination were illustrated as the object, piece-of-furniture-to-be-refinished, attracted multiple horizons of meaning that transcended mere perception. Indeed, as we have seen, perception itself carries with it a dimension of depth which enables the human being to transcend straightforward sentient insertion into the world. Further exposition points toward a description of elements which ground the experiences of memory and projection that are essential to any activity.[8]

The first element is the aperture of awareness through which we grasp an immediate present. The capacity of consciousness to take an object is that power of the agent to grasp and etch out present experience. The perception of objects and other organisms, the awareness of vital processes in the body, the deliverances of memory and imagination all become objects of conscious awareness in the present by means of the self's active grasp. Those portions of experience which are bounded by the awareness of an immediate present are made continuous by the presence of additional structures. That we do not move from one flash of awareness to another in a disconnected series of present moments is explained by the fact that the image of the aperture does not refer to a circle of light illuminating first this

---

8. For Schutz's discussion of inner time consciousness, see PSW, pp. 45–63; cf. Edmund Husserl, *The Phenomenology of Inner Time-Consciousness,* ed. Martin Heidegger (Bloomington: Indiana University Press, 1964).

and then that dimension of experience. Rather, the aperture is elongated, opening in such a way that each resolution or present focus carries with it horizons standing in various shades of illumination in relation to the immediate present. In terms of our example, what must be explained is this: How are we able to recall that we sanded the piece of furniture yesterday, that we intend to stain it today, and that we will varnish it as we had previously imagined in our initial project?

As each present phase of any experience is focused by the aperture of awareness, it immediately begins to sink into the twilight, soon to be lost below the level of consciousness. But we find that experiences are not lost, but rather are sedimented in thematic layers which bear some correspondence to the original experience. These thematic layers can be awakened and can rise up in the form of experience in the memorial mode. The reason why phases of present experience are relatively continuous, and seem to be at hand even after they have been "forgotten," is grounded in the capacity to retain immediately past phases of experience. In a dialogue, for example, we grasp the afterimages of a presently unfolding conversation. If we misunderstand a phrase or fail to grasp the meaning of a gesture, we may say to our partner, "Wait, stop right there! Repeat what you said just a moment ago."

Previously elapsed experience which is set off, thematized, and sedimented forms the material for more complex acts of recollection. Turning back upon previously elapsed experience recalls sedimentations from the darkness of unawareness into the light of a reflective present, and experience becomes filled with present images of the self's past. The capacity to turn back upon sedimented or just-past phases of experience is dependent upon the primary thrust of consciousness. That the material of memory is at hand depends upon routine interpretation, which means typification, of experience and its sedimentation. The accumulative character of experience, as the self grows and matures, depends precisely upon the grasp, retention, and thematic layering that proceeds in ordinary experience in a taken-for-granted manner.

As has been pointed out, thematic layers which form the content of sedimented experience correspond to some extent to the original lived experience. And, in addition to this, these themes are typified according to the kind of experience that was endured. The basic categories of experience, such as dreams, fantasies, practical acts, and so on, have a particular cultural order which will be discussed at a later point. The main thing to notice here is that once the cultural order has been established in language, sedimentation at the individual level proceeds by ordering experiences according to their type, whether dreams, fantasies, play, moral experience, scientific reflection, or religious ecstasy.[9] The objects of our recollective grasp normally appear on the horizon of memory according to the order by which they have been interpreted. In other words, we recall that we refinished a piece of furniture, but we do not normally recall the piece of furniture as an object in a dream world—unless we actually have had a dream in which this object played a primary role.

This account of memory is essential to the activity of interpretation which will play a central role in an understanding of moral experience. Turning toward sedimented experiences involves routine or self-conscious acts of interpretation as the self attempts to survey the past in the light of its possible significance. If we focus for the moment upon self-conscious interpretation, then two aspects of this activity become important.[10] First is the way the self grasps the meaning of past experiences in a single glance, by which the total configuration of elapsed experience is apprehended in its unity and complexity. "Yes," we say to ourselves, "the primary meaning of my gift of the piece of furniture was to preserve a sense of continuity between the generations." Separate phases of the project and the alternative projects which were at times at the center of attention are all absorbed into a primary interpretation. In such cases the memorial horizon stands out as a significant whole in relation to other dimensions of experience. A second modality occurs when the glance of the agent appears in the form of several acts which

9. Schutz, SLW, pp. 122-24.
10. Ibid., pp. 53-54.

rehearse in imagination various phases that made up the elapsed experience. In contrast with the single thematic glance, this more complicated interpretative process may be motivated by the emergence of disturbances of self-interpretation which stimulate the rehearsal of the past in such a way that the parts of experience are retraced and their meaning perhaps reconfigured.

This last point opens toward a fundamental dimension of the freedom of human agents. This is a freedom which is inherent in both biographical horizons of experience and the horizons that constitute the social world. There is an ongoing sedimentation of experience which proceeds routinely, but dialectically related to this is the capacity to transcend experience by turning back upon it. Each act of recollection is both an elongation of the aperture of awareness toward horizons of sedimented experience and fundamentally a new act, an act which may give rise to reinterpretation of the past as it has been grasped previously by the self. This means that the past has both the character of recognizable identity in the experience of agents and potentially open horizons. The open horizons are made possible by the capacity to turn back upon experience in acts of recollection and through these acts to reconstitute its meaning in various ways. At a later point we will examine how reinterpretation may occur at the level of the social world.

The self as agent not only experiences a sense of the past through the acts we have described; the self as agent also presses into the future. To continue the earlier analogy, this thrusting forward of consciousness is an elongation of the aperture of awareness toward a horizon which is more like a dawning sky than the twilight of receding experience. This structure of expectation is the ground upon which the agent's projective activity rests; and it is dialectically related to the grasp by which each passing phase of experience is retained. In all of its projective activity the self as agent fills in experience with concrete images of the future. Whether these images have to do with such mundane activities as refinishing a piece of furniture or with the realization of a complicated moral project, they all require that basic capacity of consciousness through which a sense of the future arises. In this mode the self transcends the stream of awareness, not by turning back against it, but rather by leaping forward in imagination to a state of affairs which is not yet. Such imagined states of affairs may lure the self toward their realization through appropriate forms of action.

Imagining alternative futures which fill in the basic structure of expectation is a process which, like reinterpreting the past, points toward another dimension of human freedom. Both reinterpreting the past and imaging alternative futures require open horizons as a condition of possibility. If the concrete horizons of memory and the anticipated future were absolutely fixed, then there would be no freedom for the self. There is a fragility, an instability, about these horizons which renders them fluid and filled with potentiality to be realized in fresh acts of interpretation and projection.

Perhaps enough has been said to introduce a view of how the self as agent articulates experience in terms of past, present, and future. We have shown that these dimensions are made possible by structural features that are essential to consciousness in its human form. It should be emphasized again that the experiences of past, present, and future are actually interpenetrating. They wax and wane as the self attends to experience now in the memorial mode, now in the mode of the future, and now as being absorbed in present activity. That the self is never immersed exclusively in any one dimension is due to the fact that internal time consciousness describes features of a single human reality as it is articulated in various ways. Absorption in present practical activity carries with it meaning horizons related to typical interpretations of the past and expected images of the future; even though these may be beyond the grasp of conscious awareness, they still are operative and fill out the self's essential temporality.

The capacity of consciousness to take an object, the grasp of a present, turning back upon experience in memory, and envisioning worlds that are not yet are unique elements of human transcendence. We have described the essential structures which make these more complex acts possible, and we have traced them to their ground in the spontaneity of consciousness. These achievements of transcendence give form to a prereflective running off of experience which is never fully captured by the focusing aperture of awareness. As long as consciousness exists, there is a deep sensibility of being carried irreversibly forward, a running off of experience which is completed only at death.[11]

The acts by which agents transcend and give form to this primordial stream are, according to this analysis, constitutive of meaning in human experience. Indeed, the acts that have been described up to this point are acts which give rise to meaning; the objects paired with these acts, whether they are concerned with a practical project, a memory, a fantasy, or a dream, are nothing other than meanings intended by acts of consciousness. The human agent is viewed as a center from which meaning arises, through which meaning is preserved, and in response to whose acts meanings are transformed. As we will come to understand, human agents are also beings who share horizons of meaning and in this manner give rise to a social world. The point to be emphasized here is that, without denying that there is an object world in a purely physical sense, the perception, memory, and imagination of human agents are never concerned with objects other than in terms of their meaning. To make the point more sharply, the content of the experience of human agents is entirely of the character of intended meanings.[12] This point will be elaborated further as the argument unfolds in the following chapters.

EMBODIMENT

If not further qualified, the analysis as it has evolved up to this point might lead to the view that the conscious experience of human agents is universal and disembodied. To the contrary, human conscious experience is both finite and embodied. The

---

11. Schutz, PSW, pp. 45–47. The figure of a stream employed below is derived from William James. See Schutz, "William James' Concept of the Stream of Thought, Phenomenologically Interpreted," CP, Vol. III, pp. 1–14.

12. Schutz, PSW, pp. 69–71. I accept Schutz's view that meaning arises in acts of interpretation which involve turning back upon experience; I extend this notion to include acts that grasp and etch out present objects as well as acts that project possible objects or courses of action. In this view, meaning is related to all three dimensions of internal time consciousness.

image of agency which we are developing must include as one of its foundations the reality of the flesh, for to be conscious is to be interpenetrated with desire. This affective source of experience, when interpreted, is a horizon of meaning which may empower action in a multitude of ways. At this point we need to trace out a general perspective on the agent as embodied creature.[13]

To have a body is, first, to have a center from which all action and experience proceed. It is, in the second place, to be limited by the circle which the body draws around all possible and actual acts and experiences. Finally, to have a body is to have desire at the core of conscious experience. The agent is understood, then, as embodied, and radically so, in these three senses: action and experience are centered in the body as locus and medium; action and experience are limited by the circle of the body, but are opened up by human capacities for transcendence; action and experience are grounded dialectically in desire. An elaboration of these three points will fill out and deepen the description of the self as agent.

The body which enfolds conscious experience is, first, a condition of possibility rather than a limitation. If the reality of embodiment is conceived in terms of a unity of flesh and consciousness rather than as an alien principle, then the possibility of the body as a medium of action and experience becomes clearer. All that has been described up to this point finds its focus and release in the embodied self. The complex articulations in inner time require the medium of the body in order for inner time to make its way into the social world. The projected vision of a piece-of-furniture-to-be-refinished would remain at the level of fantasy without the medium of the body. Bodily skills and movements are essential to the realization of this and other human projects.

Conceived strictly at the organic level, the medium of the

---

13. The treatment here does not pretend to be a complete or even an adequate phenomenology of embodiment. For an illuminating discussion of this issue, see Richard M. Zaner, *The Problem of Embodiment: Some Contributions to a Phenomenology of the Body* (The Hague: Martinus Nijhoff, 1964).

body is required for the flowering of consciousness as we have described it. The great body systems, the flow of vital fluids, the deliverance of oxygenated blood to the central nervous system, the ingestion and processing of food in proper quantity and quality, the maintenance of an appropriate environment—all are presupposed as foundations for the intentional operations of consciousness. Although this argument maintains a dialectical relationship between consciousness and body, avoiding a reduction of consciousness to the status of an epiphenomenon of a more basic biological process, the interdependence is deep and final. There is no agency, no intentional awareness, without body. The living consciousness which is central to an understanding of agency is presented incarnate, and thus in a mediated fashion.

The body is also the center in relation to which we experience the world, interpreting its dimensions in terms of our embodied position.[14] For example, we may, through bodily movements, transpose ourselves from one location to another. The "here" which we vacated becomes a "there" and the previously defined "there" now becomes our "here." When we have moved from a here to a there, the same acts of perception, imagination, and recollection continue to constitute any particular present as this present "now" in our experience. The point is that bodily movement induces perspectival and even interpretative shifts due to the changes in horizon that are entailed. Consider the common experience of walking through an area that was previously familiar only from the perspective of an automobile. The arrangement of streets, lawns, and houses obviously does not change; but the shift in perspective brought about by walking rather than driving can have a striking effect upon experience and interpretation.

Perspectival shifts also have an impact upon the contouring of internal time, which affects the way we experience the meaning of the objects we intend. For example, bodily movements, such as "going on vacation," may have quite a radical impact upon our images of identity and the future, as well as give us

14. Schutz, CP, Vol. I, pp. 222-26.

"perspective" upon the present. Important for this analysis are perspectival shifts, which may or may not involve bodily movements, but which do entail the imaginal entry into the experience of another person or the interpretation of the experiences of a group. Taking the point of view of the other promotes a type of moral discernment which we will take up later in an analysis of moral discourse.

Not only is the body a condition of possibility, but it is also a condition of limitation. There are obvious limits such as disease and fatigue, but we have in view the limits of bodily reality relating to the fact that it is impossible for us to act at more than one location at a time. Though we can transcend embodiment in various ways, it is not possible to act directly in more than one place at the same time. In modern society we tend to forget this limitation since we have developed so many social and technical means which allow us to act indirectly upon the world, often at many places at the same time. These modes of action will be examined in greater detail at a later point. What is to be emphasized here is that a fundamental limit is placed upon *direct* action by the body.

At a different level, though it is possible to perceive another's body and experience that other as possessing a consciousness and affectivity similar to our own, and though it is possible, through acts of communication, to enter into various forms of relationship with others, it is still impossible to *be* another. The limit of the body prevents us from exchanging places with the other in a radical sense. The body is the possibility for the focus of the intentional center which is the conscious self; and the body is also the limit which prevents a loss of centeredness through merger with the other.

Finally, the body is a limit in a still more radical sense: it contains within itself the principle of finitude, mortality. The sense of finitude is the "fundamental anxiety" which lies behind many of our life plans and projects.[15] A mature sense of selfhood emerges when signals of finitude proceeding from the body are acknowledged. In the earlier example, one of the

15. Ibid., p. 228.

possible purposes for refinishing the piece of furniture was to preserve generational continuity; this purpose could be empowered partially by feelings associated with finitude. The more general point to be derived here is that the body is the finite, affective center which energizes our recollections, present experiences, and projects. Images about the past, present experience, and projects are incarnate acts of a self capable of the full range of affectivity proceeding from the body.

Again it needs to be emphasized that this analysis holds in clear focus the dialectical relationship between embodiment and consciousness. This dialectic, when taken as primordial, enables us to avoid the twin perils of falling into a reduction of experience to its biological core, on the one hand, or to a denial of that biological core in favor of some form of idealism, on the other hand. As incarnate, the self comprehends both of these poles, and both are essential to an understanding of agency.

SOCIALITY

The stream out of which meaning arises as a consequence of acts of memory and projection and which is enfolded in bodily form is the source of our direct experience; however, the field of meaning which unfolds in internal time is a sphere which is absolutely unique for every agent and cannot be grasped directly by another. The appearance of another body in the field of my perception is paired with a reality which I experience as another human consciousness and embodied affectivity possessing capacities for experience that are articulated, as are mine, in internal time. If it is impossible to enter directly into another's stream of consciousness, then in what sense can it be argued that the agent is characterized fundamentally by sociality?

The answer to this question lies in the fact that an important capacity of agency is the ability to transcend embodied experience in various ways. This feature rests, as we have argued, in the capacity of consciousness to become paired with realities which are not directly available, in this case the reality of another center of human awareness. The pairing of the perception of another's body with that other's field of conscious experience is not a consequence of inference or analogy; it is rather a consequence of the structure of human consciousness itself. This is the formal ground which makes experiences of concrete communication among human agents possible.

Concrete human relations and interactions articulate themselves in complex networks, from the most intimate to the most anonymous relations. At this juncture we will reserve an analysis of predecessors and successors for a later treatment and comment more specifically on the world of contemporaries and their interrelationships. The most intimate of relationships among contemporaries occurs in a face-to-face context when each partner in the interaction is aware of and acknowledges in acts of communication the other's existence and stream of awareness. When the other's body is present in my field of perception and when I sense, through the process described earlier, that I am in the presence of another being with a consciousness of internal time, a biography, and so on, then the possibility for mutuality of experience is present.[16]

If we compare the nature of interactions along the continuum running from intimacy to anonymity, then further light is shed upon the nature of our sociality. In the most intimate of relationships, I am able, through acts of interpretation, to grasp the other's communications. Likewise, the other is able, through acts of interpretation proceeding from an internal time consciousness that is distinct from mine, to grasp the unfolding meanings which I attempt to communicate. This mutual "tuning in" which occurs in an intimate context of communication issues in the meshing of two distinct streams of awareness in a mutual process of interpretation and response. The meshing of two human centers is not, as we have said, a merger; but it is a vivid simultaneity of experience which emerges when my capacity to grasp and interpret another becomes mutually acknowledged by that other. This does not mean, of course, that I apprehend the other without the aid of what earlier we called types. For example, in an intimate interaction with a son or

16. This analysis is immediately influenced by Schutz's treatment of the we-relationship, PSW, pp. 163–72.

daughter, certain general meanings and expectations concerning "sons" and "daughters" will condition the experience.

As we move from intimacy to anonymity, the forms of human interaction take on more the character of limitation and segmentation according to the nature of typified meanings under which relations occur and are interpreted. For example, the other may not fully acknowledge the uniqueness and fullness of my presence and may apprehend me under meanings associated with types, such as teacher, soldier, black, poor, and so on. These anonymous apprehensions of the other are socially constructed and widely shared meaning structures which order relations in the social world. They depend for their existence upon the continual legitimacy granted to them by the human agents who constructed them.

These remarks lead to the conclusion that human consciousness is not only directional, time-full, and embodied, but it is also intersubjective. The past is apprehended by the agent as a past which can be shared with other agents at various levels of intimacy; the world of present experience is a world which is shared in various important ways with contemporaries; the projects which agents form about the future conform to, complement, or conflict with projects in the social world; and we, along with our companions, expect that there will be those who will come after us, successors, who will experience and share a social world as peculiar to their experience as ours is to our own experience.

Furthermore, if the nature of agents is less like monads and more like an existence in copresence with others, then the character of the social world and how it is formed becomes easier to understand. From this perspective, the social world arises as a consequence of sharing meanings at such a level of depth that their reality in the experience of agents becomes massive and taken for granted. One part of this social world is composed of shared typical understandings of the meaning of objects, events, others, institutions, social relationships, and so on. These meanings are sedimented in experience and are mediated through language. Another part of the social world is composed of those meanings which transcend the taken-for-granted everyday world. These levels concern the irruption of aesthetic sensibilities, experiences of value, and religious awareness, to mention three important examples. Such experiences are made possible through the operation of symbols, which are also partly mediated through language. The symbolic is broader than language, however, and includes the media of form, color, music, gesture, and material objects, such as crosses and crescents. The social world is, then, a typical–symbolic reality, arising from the basis of features which are indigenous to the human being.

It is now time to look back over the terrain covered and assess what has been accomplished as well as anticipate what is to come. The understanding of human agency has been deepened by appealing to themes which, taken together, form the outlines of a philosophical anthropology. This view of how experience occurs, how it is articulated in inner time, how it is embodied, and how it is essentially social is relevant to an understanding of moral agency and moral experience. In this chapter the argument proceeded at a very high level of generality, and it is not entirely clear how moral agency and experience can be distinguished from agency and experience, generally conceived. The function of the next chapter is to move us closer to an understanding of how experiences of value depend upon elements of agency discussed up to this point and how they are to be distinguished from other possible experiences. If the consciousness of value and the experiential elements which proceed from such an awareness can be firmly grasped, then the analysis can be moved closer to an understanding of the self as moral agent.

II

The Experience of Value

THE SELF AS AGENT apprehends experience at various levels of depth and in terms of multiple horizons of meaning. We have explored some of the foundations upon which memorial, imaginative, and projective activities rest. What we must now bring into view is how these foundations make experiences of value possible. Value experiences, we will argue, appear as a consequence of distinctive meaning horizons which are dependent upon capacities already described but at the same time are possessed of their own relative autonomy. In short, the argument will hold that values are neither epiphenomenal in human experience nor reducible to something other than themselves. They present themselves in experience as distinctive realities, though they are dependent upon certain conditions of possibility. If this argument can be established, then we will be prepared in the next chapter to describe in greater detail the nature of moral experience and the self as moral agent.

Again an example may assist the initial reflections. Imagine yourself in an open, sunny room. Sitting before a large window, you look out upon a varied landscape. Within your experience are layered several dimensions or horizons. The window frames your immediate outlook upon broader vistas outside, but at the same time you are aware of the inner horizon of the room. Peripheral levels of awareness, both auditory and visual, indicate to you the familiarity of the room. It is your room containing objects and an arrangement which stamp it with an identity associated with your biography. But the room is not at the center of awareness, even though it could become so if an intrusive experience, such as an unfamiliar sight or sound, caused you to shift attention from the scene framed by the window to the more immediate environment of the room.

But nothing disturbs you within the room. Even though the background of your awareness is etched by a ticking clock and occasional sounds of others moving about in the house, your attention is absorbed by the scene framed by the window. The window becomes a passageway into experiences of receding horizons outside the room. You are aware of the way the gradient of the land drops sharply and is broken occasionally by ragged lines of shrubs and other sparse vegetation. Beyond the last shrub boundary, the sweep of your gaze moves on to a broad expanse of meadow stretching to the right and left as far as your peripheral vision can extend. The meadow ends in a row of trees which partly conceals a sparkling river. As your gaze fixes upon the river you become aware of its rushing movement and myriad flashes of color. Leaping water turns kaleidoscopically against the background of a midafternoon sun. The sense of the room gradually and imperceptibly fades, the ticking of the clock disappears, and the meadow becomes a slash of color. The sense of the river invades awareness and occupies the center of your experience.

Even though grasped momentarily by the river, you slowly become aware of a horizon beyond the trees bordering the opposite bank of the river and merging into a dense forest. As your vision focuses upon the forest, a dimension that was background suddenly becomes foreground. Your eye follows the forest up to where a last row of trees brushes against the massive upthrust of continental cordillera. You become aware that this penultimate horizon is bordered finally by the deep blue of a vaulted sky. The foreground of the river becomes background as the sensible field of experience is dominated by mountain and sky borders.

The scene filling your experience gradually becomes fringed by another set of images. Interpenetrating the field of perception is a dimension which, though you are hardly aware of the shift, gradually rises until it becomes the central theme of your experience. Images from this dimension crowd in until the border of the window fades and experience is filtered by an imaginal context that alters the content of perception. Although you still "see" the cordillera, it is framed now by reveries of a time before the time of present experience. This time rises to awareness in the form of a vision of ancient ice fields extending as far as the eye can see, and reaching heights which dominate and exclude all other reality. An awareness of quiet loneliness and vast stretches of glacial time invade your experience.

Then the glacier begins to recede from view, only to be replaced by visions of a primeval plain upon which huge mammoths roam and lush but unfamiliar vegetation spreads. Fascinated, you focus attention upon a low ridge of stone protruding from the dark soil in the middle of the plain. Images rush until a torrent of sight and sound fills experience. Before your inner eye the ridge trembles and the whole earth shakes as a massive uplift begins. The crust of the earth undulates. Then you see the cordillera once again, but now within the borders of a more complex interpretative context. The mountains in immediate perception have risen from the center of the earth at some ancient time, and your interpretative glance comprehends this time and the time of present perception in a single vision.

Again the theme of your awareness shifts, this time accompanied by a mild shock. The angle of the lowering sun has brought into view a variety of hues brushed across the rocky face of the uplift. Each slope of the cordillera blushes with its own color, punctuated here by the darkened slash of a gorge and there by wind-and-water-sculpted features carved into stone and soil. Form and color shimmer in experience and you are grasped by a rush of aesthetic sensibilities filling perception and reverberating affectively in imagination.

Then still another horizon intercepts your experience, appearing first in vague sensibilities and then in increasingly clear images. Its content has finally to do with groping toward comprehension of the beauty and terror of your experience. At the center of consciousness, questions of purpose and cause haunt the field of perception with an additional horizon of meaning. What is the nature of such beauty and power flowing into experience through the passageway of a window? What does this power mean for your life and the lives of your companions? Is the force which pulsates in your vision and at the center of consciousness the same power? Is it a principle that is alien to you and your kind, or is it beneficient? Is it a force that is ultimately good, or is it an unthinking, destructive, and evil force which, though productive of wonder and beauty, will finally swallow all in death?

The wings of a hawk slice through this last gossamery horizon. A ticking clock becomes increasingly audible and the sounds of the house make their way into consciousness. The window merges back into the wall as shapes and objects of the room come into focus. You become aware of the smells of cooking food. A glance through the window, now seemingly smaller and less luminous, reveals that the angle of the sun has become sharply more acute, allowing dusky blues and purples to creep across the river and gradually up the cordillera. In a language familiar to you, full of rumbles and groans, your body delivers a message which becomes increasingly thematic, generating a number of routine movements and projects—you are hungry.

MIGRATIONS OF EXPERIENCE

Experiences such as I have described are mundane possibilities for consciousness in its human form. They have manifold nuances, and the material content of experience may vary widely among individuals and between cultures. This variation of experience is grounded in features which provide the conditions of possibility for the migrations that have been described. If we begin with the observation that we do move, in the course of daily life, through several distinguishable orders of experience, then one plausible hypothesis which partly explains such common migrations is this: human conscious experience appears in the form of a continuum upon which first this, then that horizon is accented. The nature of the focus of conscious attention is, from this perspective, the regulative principle determining which horizon will thematize experience at what point on the continuum. An additional perspective which further strengthens the argument holds that what is accented as real for the self depends upon the focus of conscious attention. What is thematized at the center of experience and the sense of reality with which it is accented are both dependent upon focusing acts of attending consciousness.[1] If we apply these perspectives to the initial example, some illumination follows.

It becomes clear, for example, that the acts of perception described received a particular focus which is related to the regulative function of attention. Had the room been the focus, then other possibilities would have been excluded. The window would have remained a window rather than becoming, as it did, a passageway into other orders of experience. It might have provided light and perhaps warmth, but the nature of attention would have limited experience to the horizon of the room. Within the room it is possible that other experiences could take place: a conversation with a close friend, entering imaginatively into a world presented by a novel, mastering a puzzle in mathematics, listening to music, making love, and so on. The point is that these experiences are only possibilities as long as the focus of attention remains as it was described; this and only this series of experiences was actualized. Likewise, it is clear that the sense of subjective reality could have been accented differently. I could "live out of" the world of a novel, contemplate a difficult problem, or fantasize a series of acts which would lead me to the home of my lover or to the preparation of a delicious meal. But none of these senses of reality characterized the example.

Though suggestive, these remarks do not take us far enough. We do not know, for example, how to describe the differences that seem to characterize these various levels of experience. In order to bring this problem into clear focus, let us return to the initial example and trace in the background of what was ex-

---

1. This entire chapter is influenced by the analysis of Alfred Schutz which appears in his essay, "On Multiple Realities," CP, Vol. I, pp. 207–59. I consider my treatment of issues in this chapter to be a constructive appropriation of Schutz rather than an exposition, especially since I am primarily interested in value meanings, a problem which was not of central concern to him.

perienced in greater detail. It is clear that in order to have such an experience, some of the main features discussed in the first chapter have to be presupposed. Conscious experience is directional and embodied; the experience unfolds in inner time; forms of transcendence, such as turning back upon experience in acts of interpretation, were present; and the entire experience was grounded in social embodiment.

The various migrations which the experience illustrates also highlight the concurrence and successive dominance of distinct orders of meaning. The first and most obvious of these levels has to do with the perception of a world which included the inner horizon of the room and the outer horizon of meadow, river, mountains, and sky. The "here" of embodiment imparted a quality to the experience which would have been different if, for example, the experience had been determined by a locus on the river or in the mountains.

A second level appeared with the self's active engagement in a world of meaning projected in imagination. The beginning of the imaginal process occurred when meadow, river, and mountains receded from view and were replaced by reveries about origins. That imagination portrayed an inner scene concerning the origins of mountains and prehistoric conditions is not arbitrary, because the content of imagination could have been otherwise. It was configured in just this manner as a consequence of two elements which interpenetrate each other. One of these elements is the biography of the experiencing person and the other is the social world. Let us suppose that the person has had a long fascination with the geologic formation of the earth and has, furthermore, spent a great deal of time in the mountains. The content of imagination will be shaped by these biographical interests and previously sedimented experiences. Likewise, in the social world there are a number of sedimented traditions of interpretation concerning the origin of the mountains which were the subject of initial perception. The content of imagination will also be formed by typical interpretations that the individual has assimilated from the social world.

A third level appeared when the experience of imagining a

time before the time of present perception gradually faded to be replaced by a dawning awareness of color and form. The appearance of this theme at the center of consciousness signals entry into a dimension of aesthetic meaning. The mode of experience is still imaginal, but the content of imagination is filled not with visions of a past geological time, but rather with combinations of various colors. Entry into such experiences could be characterized by the figure of a "leap" as well as by a gradual process of rising awareness. Whether the person is shocked by a sudden aesthetic awareness, or becomes gradually conscious of a difference in experience, the point is that a theme change has taken place. It is no longer the taken-for-granted world or the biographically specific imaginal world which is thematized in experience; the world now presents itself as a thing of beauty.

A fourth level rose when the experience of beauty was represented as evoking not only aesthetic sensibilities but also wonder and awe. In this instance, the example portrayed experience as involving the act of turning back upon just-past perceptions and imaginal meanings, subjecting them to interpretation. These acts of interpretation drove experience toward two possible regions of meaning, the evaluative and the religious. Just how these regions are related, or whether they interpenetrate in some manner, is not clear from the example. It is clear that interpretative struggles concerning the goodness or evil of the power sensed in the vision of mountains involve value meanings which perhaps are fringed with religious meanings.

Finally, at its most basic level, acts of interpretation which approached aesthetic, evaluative, and religious levels of meaning were essentially dependent upon the presence of symbols that evoked meanings transcending the surface elements of experience. We will have to attend, in the next chapter, to the ways in which different sets of symbols, imbedded in the social world and mediated intersubjectively, are capable of evoking different experiences of value. At this point, however, it is only necessary to establish sufficient support for the argument that the experience of value (and, by extension, aesthetic and religious experience) is made possible by granting the accent of reality to a province of value meanings which then comes to thematize experience in determinate ways.

VALUE MEANINGS

Even though we have a general view of the possibilities of experiential migration, and we now understand something of how experiences of value occur, the nature of value meanings themselves is still unclear, and especially how they can be distinguished from other meanings. Further analysis of the nature of the objects of our awareness and the acts which give rise to these objects will shed light upon this problem.

When we recall that what is meant by "object of experience" is the way a conscious subject attends to and thematizes experience, then what we are talking about are horizons of meaning which texture experience in various ways. There is a difference between the mountain as perceived, mountain as the theme of a dream, mountain as an object of imagination, and mountain as a project. In each of these cases, mountain appears in experience as belonging to a different meaning structure or order of objects; and each of these orders of objects appears to be correlated with different acts of conscious awareness.

To continue with the illustration, the acts of perception that initially mark off the mountain in experience from trees, river, and so on, are acts that give rise to a particular order of objects. Taken as a whole, this class of objects comprises the meaning structure of an intersubjective, sensible world. This world is deeply affected by our position, and all objects which appear within its horizon are apprehended under the sign of embodiment. Experience is also deeply conditioned by an unquestioned presupposition. We take for granted that the mountain that is perceived today will be the same mountain that will be perceived tomorrow and that was perceived yesterday. Meanings which are embedded in typical form in language indicate that we interpret the objects of our perceptual experience as having a continuing "empirical" identity.

By contrast, when the mountain appears as the object of acts of memory, we are in the presence of a different order of meaning. Both the order of objects in the mode of memory and the acts that make them possible are different. No longer are we dealing with objects grasped by acts of perception; rather, we are dealing with acts of imagination which turn back upon sedimented meanings, bringing the mountain-as-remembered into the center of awareness. The meaning of mountain as an object of memory is distinct because it involves acts of imagination that reconstitute typified experience rather than acts of perception that thematize presently unfolding experience. Furthermore, the identity of mountain-as-remembered is not of the same order as mountain-as-perceived. In the case of memory, identity and continuity are typical rather than perceptual; the difference is between the identity of sensible objects grasped in perception and the identity of typified experience which becomes the object of conscious recollection. Mountain-as-remembered also appears upon the horizon of the past as etched out within internal time, rather than appearing within the meaning context of clock time of the everyday world that measured the various outlooks toward the mountain as it was grasped in perception. Further similarities and differences appear when the mountain becomes the object of a project. The similarity with memory comes at the point of sedimented typifications which are portrayed in imagination. Identity is still at the level of typicality, but the sense of time is characterized by imagining in the "future perfect tense." The mountain becomes the object of imaginal acts that are projected as if they had already happened.

If we apply the foregoing analysis to the problem of value, then it is possible to see that value meanings arise as a dimension associated with the experience of other objects of awareness. For example, value meanings may arise as a dimension of acts of memory, as a horizon fringing projects, as a layer of significance haloing objects of perception, or as a component in a process of interpretation. The claim is, however, that value meanings are not reducible to memory, projects, perception, and so on. The problem is still how to describe the distinctive character of values as they appear in connection with other dimensions of meaning.

A central theme, which discloses the nature of this difference, is found in the previous argument about human capacities for transcendence. On one level we showed that transcendence is made possible through acts of grasping experience in its dimensions of depth, by turning back upon it in acts of interpretation, and by leaping forward in acts of projection. At a deeper level we argued that transcendence is made possible by symbolic pairing of an object, event, or other that appears within the meaning horizon of the everyday world with dimensions of meaning which transcend that world. In the initial example, meanings associated with beauty, religion, and value were symbolically paired with the mountain as perceived and imagined. Once symbolic pairing has occurred, value meanings may appear as a dimension of the activities of interpreting, projecting, and so on. Value meanings are objects distinguished by their transcendent character, and they arise as a consequence of the symbolic capacities of the human being. In short, value meanings are objects of symbolic awareness. At this level, value meanings are grounded in the same formal elements as are the two other great symbolic dimensions of transcendence: art and religion. And because symbolic capacities are essential and not extrinsic to the human being, aesthetic, religious, and value experiences are not reducible to something other than themselves. They are perennial expressions of that which is essential to the human being and the human social world.

Capacities for transcendence through symbols are related to another element which gives further substance to our understanding of the nature and distinctiveness of value meanings. This element has to do with the incompleteness of the human agent. We have previously argued that the human agent is both finite and embodied; the stream of experience runs off, and horizons of meaning which give it structure appear within dimensions of inner time; but the resolution of any given experiential horizon is unstable, fragile. This essential fragility is dialectically related to symbolic capacities for transcendence. The agent which is limited, finite, and fragile has capacities for experiencing horizons of transcendent meaning in value, religion, and art. Value meanings, in particular, open up toward visions of completeness, wholeness, and rectitude. Again it is impossible to make a radical distinction between value meanings and those which make aesthetic and religious experience possible, since they share the same formal ground. All three classes of objects presuppose symbolic capacities, and it is this quality that gives them their distinctiveness in relation to other objects of experience. But in the final analysis the good, the true, and the beautiful are interpenetrating forms of human transcendence that can only be distinguished, never separated. Although the reasons for this may be clear given the analysis of human symbolic capacities, there may also be a more fundamental explanation for their final unity. But such an explanation is beyond the scope of this analysis.

ACCENT OF REALITY

We made the claim earlier that what comes into experiential focus and how objects are accented in terms of their reality is dependent upon the nature of conscious attention. We argued further that migrations of experience are characterized by alterations among different orders of objects which arise as a consequence of different acts of consciousness. We then applied these perspectives to the problem of the distinctiveness of meaning horizons associated with experiences of value. The emphasis of this section is upon the issue of what gives any dimension of experience a different sense of reality from any other. An understanding of this problem will further illuminate the view of value meanings we are developing.

The first point which needs to be emphasized is that the capacity to accent the reality of experience is not the power of a monad, but rather that of a social being. In addition, this power is not articulated in any particular ordering of experience which is absolutely prescribed. The fact that agents are embodied creatures grants a certain primacy to the shared everyday world which is within reach and upon which we act. But even in this case there is no absolute determination by any one order of the total sense of reality. To put this contention into more concrete terms, there is no reason in the nature of experience that the objects of a dream world, the objects of fantasy, the objects of everyday experience, the objects of evaluations, and so on should be arranged in a certain fixed manner concerning their experiential reality. Because we are social beings, the tendencies to accent these experiences according to a certain order appears partly as a consequence of sedimented recipes in the social world. For example, some cultures have placed greater emphasis upon the reality sense of objects, which appear as a consequence of symbolic pairing, than upon those arising out of acts of perception. In the latter case, the "material world" is reality-dominant in experience, whereas in the former case the "spiritual world" receives the dominant accent of reality. Or, again, for many in the West the reality sense of dreams is interpreted according to a scientific paradigm which reduces the dream experience to another meaning horizon, such as the psychoanalytic perspective. By contrast, for many Native Americans the reality of dreams is still connected in experience with the acquisition of sacred power.[2] In these two cases, the reality sense of dreams is accented differently, and the way it is accented depends in part on the cultural context.

Within any given biographical and social context the possible dimensions within which experience may occur and the particular order which characterizes them is partly a matter of social legitimation and partly a matter of conscious acts by individuals. It is possible, for example, to "live out of" a particular dramatic world of meaning, such as that mediated in a play or novel. Or it is possible to grant the accent of reality so totally to a realm of scientific meaning that much of experience is interpreted through the lens of scientific vision. Or it is possible to allow horizons of value meaning to fringe realms of experience in such a way that other experiential modes are subor-

---

2. See, for example, the powerful description of the importance of dreams and vision in John G. Neihardt, *Black Elk Speaks* (Lincoln: University of Nebraska Press, 1961). In my work among the Blackfeet, a plains tribe, I have been impressed by the way experiences of all sorts, including dreams, are viewed through categories which are pre-Freudian. Among these people, the sense of subjective reality is often accented in ways that are surprisingly different from those of the dominant society. For a fascinating analysis of the problem of subjective reality, see Schutz, "Don Quixote and the Problem of Reality," CP, Vol. II, pp. 135–58.

dinated to a certain set of value meanings. In the course of the experience of agents, however, migrations of consciousness usually occur in such a fashion that first this and then that dimension of meaning commands attention, and the accent of reality is granted only provisionally.

The important factor which legitimates the continual reality status of dreams, fantasy, practical life, or any other dimension is the degree to which the province is socially legitimated and shared. If a horizon of value meaning mediates a sense of its reality to individuals, and if that experience is shared, then an individual act granting the accent of reality to the experience of value receives its confirmation in the social world. We will take up this theme in greater detail at a later point, but it is necessary at least to introduce it in order to fill out our understanding at this level. The point to be emphasized is that when the accent of reality is granted at both the levels of agency and social world, then living out of a dimension of meaning may, for the duration of the experience, render other meaning horizons subordinate or even unreal. Entering a world of religious vision, being grasped by a sensibility of value, or being captured in a structure of dramatic meaning may be so powerful that other experiences are pushed to the boundaries of awareness and lose their special sense of reality, at least for the moment.

Human beings are migratory creatures and the boundaries among provinces of meaning as well as the senses of experiential reality generated by them are not fixed horizons, but rather fluid in character. In experience, any given horizon of meaning does not usually categorically exclude all the others. But one province of meaning that has been paramount may become an "enclave" within another horizon of meaning that has succeeded it in experience.[3] The example with which we began this chapter illustrates both the fluidity of the boundaries among meaning horizons and also the occasional dominance by one horizon of the sense of experiential reality. Any of these dimensions could become an enclave within another province. If we take the experience of color and form as mediated in the

---

3. On the problem of enclaves, see Schutz, CP, Vol. I, pp. 245, 233n.

aesthetic vision of the cordillera and subject it to analysis from the point of view of a theory of color and form, then what was primarily an aesthetic experience becomes an enclave within a province of theoretical thinking. Or if we take the experience of value and subject it to a process of interpretation in the light of a value theory, then primary value experience becomes an enclave within a province of theoretical thinking about ethics.

An additional dimension of the problem of enclaves will be instructive for this argument. To take the initial example once again, if we respond to smells of food and sensations of hunger, then a set of routine projects will begin to structure our attention and inform our action. The theme of our conscious lives shifts. The experiences which were reality-dominant earlier are displaced by practical activities, such as moving from the room to another part of the house, washing our hands, discussing a problem with one of our children, assisting with dinner, and so on. Even though we may be absorbed in a whole range of practical activities, the sense of wonder and power symbolically mediated in the vision of the cordillera may remain as a shadowy enclave in experience. If the experience of the horizon of value meanings has been so powerful that we cannot fully escape its memory, then we may remain unsettled and uncomfortable for a time. We may even seek consciously to return to these experiences of symbolically mediated meaning, attempting to recapture sensibilities that were displaced by entry into the everyday world with all its projects.

In the light of this analysis, it ought to be clear that the sense of experience as value-laden occurs when we grant the accent of reality to a province of value meanings and when that reality sense is confirmed in the social world. If the experience of value and its social correlate are continuing and powerful, then other ways of construing the world may diminish and even seem unreal for a time. Though the theme of awareness may shift from a horizon of value to another dimension of meaning, it is possible that the experience of value may remain as a shadow at the edges of consciousness. The enclave may be such that its power will continue to exert a certain influence over other dimensions of conscious experience.

THEMATIC CHANGE

Although we have alluded to some of the factors that explain why migrations of experience occur, this problem is not yet entirely clear. It is important that this issue receive more extended treatment because of its impact upon our understanding of why themes in experience change or, more radically, may disappear from view. In the light of the analysis in the previous section it is possible to understand generally how certain individuals and even entire cultures accent the reality of experience in a certain manner. The implications this view has for the issue of the reality sense of value meanings are also clearer. Value meanings appear at the center of awareness when their reality is accented by individual acts which are confirmed in the social world. In this section we need to attend more specifically to some of the factors that condition theme changes.

To begin at a very rudimentary level, specific themes of our conscious awareness may shift because attention is interrupted by the imposition of a different theme upon experience. Suppose we are in the midst of experiencing the cordillera in an evaluative mode and that we are suddenly interrupted by a loud noise (a gun shot?) or by the entry of another person into the room. In either case, our attention may be completely interrupted and new themes will be imposed upon our experience. At another level, before the experience of the cordillera occurred, in all of its richness and complexity, another theme may have intervened and prevented the experience from unfolding at all. For example, had an object in the room been overturned or out of place when we entered, then the theme of our conscious attention may have become the solution of the problem, "How did the chair get turned over or placed in this unfamiliar manner?"

Once our attention has been interrupted, we may seek to return to the experience, especially if it is an enclave which invites further exploration. In the case of our example, suppose we are motivated to recapture the experience and we return to the room and sit before the same window, but the window seems now only a window and does not open up as a passageway into the experience we desire to recapture. We may seek, through imaginative recollection, to waken the elements that originally informed our sense of beauty and value. This activity illustrates a voluntary attempt to shift the theme of our experience from the everyday world of familiar objects to horizons of transcendent meaning.

At a more complicated level, themes of our conscious lives shift as a consequence of symbolic pairing among different meaning horizons. For example, it is a fairly common experience that participation in a religious ritual may evoke more than one horizon of meaning. The words spoken in homily and liturgy, the songs which are shared, the art and other objects, such as crosses and chalices, the eucharist, the prayers—all are part of a multivalent field of interlocking symbols that have the capacity to evoke multiple levels of meaning in the experience of individuals.

The question at this juncture concerns factors that condition theme changes which are due to the operation of symbolic pairing. Three dimensions of this problem are especially pertinent to our analysis: first, theme changes that occur without our active attention; second, theme changes that are the consequence of a process of gradual wakening and rising up to the center of awareness; and, finally, theme changes that shock our sensibilities with a sudden shift in meaning structure.[4]

Theme changes that unfold without our active attention usually signal the presence of deeply shared symbol sets which routinely evoke in experience multiple horizons of meaning. Routinized symbol sets and their corresponding meaning horizons are easier to discern in social groups characterized by relative stability and homogeneity. In pluralistic, heterogeneous societies routinized symbols may be uncovered as a part of the experience of subgroups, but it is more difficult to locate root symbols which organize the experience of the entire society. In our own society there is presently a struggle over a number of

---

4. Schutz deals with these problems in terms of his notion of relevance. See SLW, pp. 182–229, and PR. We will return to these considerations again in Chapter IV.

major social issues; at its deepest level this struggle may be interpreted as a series of conflicts between meaning structures evoked by different symbol sets which are routinized in the experience of individuals belonging to different subgroups.

Now the claim is that in groups within which symbols are deeply routinized, individuals will undergo multiple levels of experience without taking thought; only when conflicts emerge will routinized symbols and their corresponding meaning horizons become the subject of explicit attention. If the argument is not entirely clear, then further appeal to the illustration with which we began the chapter will perhaps bring it into focus. Recall that the experience as it was described had a particular shape which was dependent upon specific typical and symbolic horizons. It could have been otherwise, and would have been so had instrumental symbols been deeply routinized. Had this been the case, then the view opening through the passageway of the window may have evoked in experience a sense of the possible instrumental goods that could be realized; we could imagine a campground, or better, the development of cabins with electricity and plumbing facilities on the meadow facing the river. The river, being unpolluted and full of fish, could become a prime attraction for tourists. And the mountains, with their animal life and abundant snow, could become the object of multiple projects, such as hunting, skiing, and so on. Clearly, this is a different apprehension of value from that which was initially described. Its horizon appears as a consequence of symbol sets that are not only different from those which characterized the alternative view but are also deeply routinized in the experience of many persons in our society.

Theme changes that are associated with a wakening process which gradually rises up toward the center of experience may also be illustrated by extending the initial example. As the experience unfolded, the vision of the cordillera as object of perception became paired, through symbolic means, with aesthetic, religious, and value meanings. The migrations of experience were not entirely taken for granted, and thus the symbols that wakened various experiential horizons were not completely routinized. These horizons rose up gradually, and in some instances almost imperceptibly, until the experiencing person was aware that a theme change had taken place.

Theme changes that involve an irruption of meaning horizons which depends upon a pairing of objects with strange or unfamiliar meanings points toward the multivalency and instability of symbol systems. The shock of a shift of theme due to the irruption of an unexpected meaning horizon is a familiar experience, but it is based upon a complicated set of circumstances. Experience of the cordillera as an object which either routinely evokes a sense of value meanings or gradually wakens such horizons is related to sedimentations at the levels of biography and social world. The individual who experiences the cordillera in such a manner has learned, at some past time, that objects and events in nature are important and may have a significance that transcends the everyday world. Such knowledge has been socially mediated by significant others within a communal context. The sedimented materials, carried by types and evoked by symbols, make possible the experience of symbolic meaning as a dimension of perception of the cordillera.

A shock in experience may occur when dimensions of meaning are unexpectedly paired with objects with which they are not normally associated. It may be, for example, that we are more familiar with horizons of value meaning proceeding from the social world than with those which may be evoked in a vision of nature. We may not be at all surprised by horizons of value meaning symbolically evoked by a familiar political leader (John F. Kennedy), a moral leader (Martin Luther King), or a moral project (the War on Poverty), but we may be greatly surprised by a cordillera that becomes related to an unfamiliar horizon of value meanings which suddenly irrupts into experience. In such instances we are motivated to engage in more self-conscious acts of interpretation.

In cases when routine symbols and those that are sufficiently shared to waken experience in large numbers of individuals are operating, we are usually in the presence of relative social stability. Appropriate migrations of experience within a socially legitimated order recur again and again in the experience of individuals. Theme changes may occur as a consequence of the creative instability of symbol systems, and new horizons of meaning may irrupt into individual experience in such a manner as to stimulate social change. Themes disappear when the relationship between symbol sets and the experiences they mediate begin to break down. When this occurs, we are in the presence of widespread social change, which may result finally in a shift in the root paradigms by which individuals and social groups interpret their identity and destiny. In these cases, a search begins for cultural traditions that can be reinterpreted in such a way that new images of identity and destiny may arise.

The major parts of the argument in this chapter may now be brought together. The human agent, we have claimed, apprehends the world in terms of multiple horizons of meaning. The accent of reality may be granted to one (or more) of these horizons, and the self may live out of it (or them) for a time. Migration among dimensions of meaning is, at the level of value experience, made possible by the operation of symbols; and values become, from this viewpoint, meaning-correlates of symbolic capacities. The reality of an experience of value arises when the accent of reality is granted to a particular region of value meanings. Likewise, the experience of value is muted, subordinated, and may even disappear altogether if a theme shift occurs in individual experience or in the social world. We will extend this analysis in the next chapter in such a way that our understanding will move closer to a view of the self as moral agent.

III

The Self as Moral Agent

THE FIRST TWO CHAPTERS have focused on elements of agency that are essential to understanding the moral life. In the preceding chapter the formal ground upon which the experience of value arises was described, and it is the task of this chapter to analyze horizons of value meaning that have more specific content. Such an exploration will illustrate the way in which different value horizons evoke different moral sensibilities as well as expose more clearly the universal anthropological ground out of which these value horizons emerge. Before proceeding directly to this analysis, an important distinction, alluded to in the last chapter, must be recalled.[1]

This distinction basically involves the difference between moral experience as it is endured by agents and the retrospective analysis of that experience. At one level, this distinction simply describes the capacity of agents to apprehend horizons of value, as well as other sorts of meaning, and to grasp these horizons retrospectively in acts of interpretation. At another level, the distinction points toward the difference between "ordinary" moral experience and interpretations of that experience which are embodied in theoretical treatments of the moral life. The intention of this analysis is to develop categories of interpretation that are adequate to the actual stuff of ordinary moral experience. As such, this treatment shares with other theoretical reflection in a certain abstraction from the stream of moral experience; but the abstraction which description requires must never be confused with the vitality and dynamism of concrete

1. See p. 48.

moral experience or with living moral traditions in the social world.[2]

Perhaps another complex example will aid in discerning the intricacies of ordinary moral experience. Imagine yourself engaged in a conversation with friends concerning the issue of nuclear energy. The initial discussion is focused by a debate between two persons in the group.

One friend vigorously defends a national policy that will increase our dependence upon nuclear energy. "Such a policy is imperative," she argues, "in order to preserve and extend our present quality of life. Our other energy sources are either diminishing or are presently under the control of increasingly hostile foreign powers. We must develop a policy which will free us from this dependence and ensure a cheap and reliable energy source for the future. If we achieve this goal, then our movement into the twenty-first century will be greatly enhanced. The cities we have developed can be adequately powered, and the individual homes within those cities can be well heated and cooled. Our cars, airplanes, and other systems of transportation can perhaps be revolutionized. In addition, we can develop even more elaborate technological means to make our lives freer and culturally much richer."

The other friend, accepting the fundamental vision of the future which has been proposed, argues a slightly different case. "I am not convinced that the issue can be stated so simply," he says. "Surely it is not the case that our social choices are between an almost absolute national dependence upon nuclear energy or an inevitable and disastrous decline in our quality of life. We certainly have more than one energy source, even if some of them will not last forever. What is wrong with developing a national policy which involves the judicious use of our coal, gas, and oil, while at the same time we seek to make our

---

2. The intention here is to develop adequate typifications of moral experience. This problem is addressed by Alfred Schutz in PSW, ch. 5. Whereas Schutz develops his views in relation to problems of interpretative sociology, I am more interested in the implications of his thought for constructive ethical reflection. I view the methodological problem of describing subjective meaning contexts as similar in both the social sciences and ethics.

nuclear plants safer? Along with this, we could explore further energy sources, develop synthetic fuels, and commit a certain amount of our national resources to the development of solar and fusion energy. Such a mixed plan will provide us with even greater security and will enable us to move in the future toward the sort of society and quality of life which both of us envision.''

At this point another friend joins the issue from a different perspective. "I think," he begins, "that both of you have failed to make a fundamental point. Part of our problem, and an essential part as I see it, is that both individuals and groups in the country cannot come to any agreement upon proper regulation of their activities. Oil companies are in competition with each other to make the most profit and to control their supplies; consumers are in competition with each other and with the companies for their own personal energy needs; and our country is in competition with other nations for world energy resources. If we could come to some agreement upon legislative principles or even laws which could restrain such destructive competition, then perhaps we could develop a system of international regulation which would be acceptable. We have an obligation in this matter, not only to one another and to other nations, but to future generations as well, in my view. We must embody these mutual obligations in appropriate rules and laws. I think that this is the most acceptable way of approaching the energy question.''

Before this position can be completely articulated, an additional voice joins the discussion. "Quality of life, indeed! That is just the problem," she exclaims. "We have created a society so dependent upon consumption that we are required, or so we believe, to dominate the earth, and even other people, in order to sustain our inordinate affluence and inflated life-styles. The earth is not ours to dominate. That is what none of you has understood up to this point. No matter what our energy needs, and I am not saying that we have none, we must learn to relate to our natural environment in a more fitting and responsible manner. We must transform the cultural values which have, up to this point, motivated us to dominate and compete. We are going to have to envision our earth as a fragile and living tissue upon which all of us are dependent, and not something that is simply passive before our incessant demands. In short, we must appropriate a vision of the earth and our resources which affirms that the environment responds to our individual and corporate actions. That means we must gauge our actions in the light of that response in ways I have failed to see us do up to this point. I believe that if we form our attitudes in this manner, then we can view the energy problem in its most adequate interpretative framework.''

"Now this argument makes a point that I have been feeling is really the most important," another friend says, joining in the conversation for the first time. "When you mention our attitudes, then I think you are moving in the right direction. What we need to do in relation to our energy needs may be something like one of you proposed earlier. I think I agree that we must develop multiple energy resources for the future; and I also agree with the view that we need to be more responsible toward our environment. But I think we do this not by obeying rules or formulating regulations but rather by developing a sense of discipline and habits of conservation. Our habits of consumption and, really, our terribly unnecessary waste are the problems. We need to adopt in our lives the discipline which will drastically change our direction as a nation. We must find ways to evoke these personal life-styles in others with whom we relate in the world and, most important, we must train our children so that they will reflect these dispositions. If we focus attention upon programs of education designed to change our life-styles, then the energy problem will largely take care of itself."

"None of you has really seen the central issue yet," a final friend objects. "It is really the consequences of our bad habits, our exploitation of the earth, and our materialistic culture which need attention. And in regard to nuclear energy, the most important outcomes have to do literally with poisoning the earth and the atmosphere, not only for ourselves, but also for future generations. Radiation poisoning has already led to increased risk of cancer in our population and to genetic defects in the unborn. If you combine this pollution with other forms which derive from the development of different energy sources, such as oil and coal, then you should be able to see that we are headed for an ecological apocalypse. In my view that danger looms much larger when you combine these effects with our dependence upon the development of nuclear weapons, which feeds into our present defense policy. I have a hard time seeing how we will long survive, given these realities."

Even though this conversation is both imaginary and incomplete, it is familiar and it does illustrate the complexities of ordinary moral experience. Each of the positions has a certain plausibility, and each can be located as a tradition of value in the social world. What we now need to do is focus more precisely upon the moral dimensions of experience as they appear in this conversation.

MORAL DIMENSIONS OF EXPERIENCE

The moral dimensions of any experience arise as a consequence of granting the accent of reality to a horizon of value meaning. The conflicts illustrated in the conversation are rooted in different sensibilities concerning the way experience is apprehended in the light of differing horizons. These conflicts are persistent because different value meanings evoke in experience a different sense of reality; and this reality sense may be co-experienced in the social world, a circumstance which will make value conflicts even more severe. Further anaylsis of the illustrative conversation will serve to clarify these points.[3]

The initial position debated by the first two persons exhibits a host of taken-for-granted value meanings. For example, there is a straightforward affirmation of the goodness of present urban-industrial life-styles and the cultural values which support them. In addition, there is an unquestioned assumption concerning the appropriateness of an instrumental-dominant relation to the en-

3. The description which follows could be discussed in terms of theorists of the moral life, such as Aristotle (teleology), Kant (deontology), H. Richard Niebuhr (responsibility), J. S. Mill (utilitarianism), and Thomas Aquinas (virtue). The purpose of the description, however, is to illuminate ordinary moral experience rather than to typify the moral life as it appears in the classical sources.

vironment. The environment and its energy sources are clearly to be in the service of extending a specific culturally conditioned life image and style.

Four other value meanings constitute the material content of this value horizon and, when granted the accent of reality, texture moral experience in specific ways. First, there is the assumption of the goodness of increased and even unlimited growth; second, there is an affirmation of the goodness of technology; third, there is the image of a society experiencing ever-increasing material and cultural abundance; and, fourth, there is a view of freedom that qualifies experience.

The first value meaning brings into experience a sense of an open future. Social problems, such as energy shortages, are viewed as temporary. Increased knowledge and sophisticated technology will be forthcoming to solve these problems if we only exercise the imagination and develop the will to commit the necessary resources to their solution. The second theme, the goodness of technology, has already come into view because it is meaning-compatible with the value of growth.

Also compatible are value meanings related to material abundance and freedom. The first of these values affirms the view that the accumulation of wealth, both material and cultural, will continue. This wealth makes possible the extension of an even more massive secondary environment, which will further expand our capacity to dominate nature. Our actions will be extended by more sophisticated tools, our ability to influence others by the development of more elaborate communications systems, and our freedom of movement enhanced by more efficient and faster transportation systems.

Each of these consequences illustrates the parameters of the experience of freedom which is evoked by this horizon of value meaning. Technology is the instrumental good that serves the end of creating a secondary environment which frees us from earlier forms of labor. We are now free to enjoy the higher values of culture, and especially the important value of leisure. Given the view of virtually unlimited technological capability, it is possible to experience human existence as transcending some of the classical definitions of finitude. Life-extending, nature-dominating technologies lure us into visions of a future which, if not qualified by immortality, is certainly experienced as more extensive than that anticipated by our predecessors.

The second position that emerged in the conversation illustrates a widespread and persistent apprehension of moral experience. Action and experience are thematized in such a way that networks of relations among persons and groups are experienced as appropriate or inappropriate, right or wrong, as they conform or fail to conform to norms, rules, principles, or law. A sense of the future was present in the example, an interpretation of the context of action was operative, and a view of the consequences of action was visible. The central image that qualified all of these elements, however, was a sense of obligation to intimate others, which was extended in the example to complex relations among contemporaries as well as generations of successors.

This horizon of value meaning evokes in experience a different sense of freedom as well. Freedom is apprehended, not as the capacity to transcend aspects of finitude through movement into the future, but rather as the capacity to conform experience to the appropriate rule, principle, or law: through obedience comes freedom. Although not strongly thematized in the example, some apprehensions of moral experience in the light of this value horizon would place great importance upon the generalizability of rules, principles, or laws. The greatest realization of moral rectitude would come precisely as action and experience are conformed to normative structures which are highly general, if not universal, in scope.[4]

The third position displays still a different sense of moral experience. This position is characterized by an explicit criticism of the cultural values and life-style of contemporary urban-industrial societies. Criticism turns upon the rejection of the instrumental-dominant image of our relationship to the environment and the proposal of an alternative image which is more relational and symbiotic. These differences and conflicts

---

4. The tendency toward giving central weight to the principle of universalizability would be characteristic of various forms of Kantian ethics.

may be made more explicit by further analysis of the value meanings most characteristic of this horizon.

Although moral action and experience are understood to be future oriented, this value horizon does not project the future in terms of unlimited growth. This latter sensibility is fundamentally qualified by the view that all of life, both biological and social, is interrelated and interdependent. The specific consequences of the unmitigated exploitation of nonrenewable energy resources and sensitive environments will lead not to material and cultural abundance, but rather to diminished and even desperate life possibilities.

Such a view dictates that individual and social action be marked by "responsibility" toward the environment and energy resources. In this context, the notion of responsibility seems to mean action which is fitting to the interpretation of the interrelated nature of all forms of life. By contrast with the competitive-dominant sensibilities of the first position, this view of moral experience apprehends freedom not as unlimited transcendence, but rather as action that is shaped by its interpreted consistency or lack of consistency with what is going on in the natural and social worlds.[5]

The fourth position articulated in the initial conversation evokes still a different texture in moral experience. Here the central image is the good person from whom good actions flow. Moral action is shaped, according to this value horizon, not by conformity to rules and principles, but rather by a habituated consistency among motives, intentions, and acts. It is the person of good or vicious character whom this value horizon holds clearly in view. As the habits of persons are good or vicious, so will be the quality of their acts.

Again, the view of freedom embodied in this value horizon and evoked in moral experience is distinguishable from those that have been described previously. Freedom is essentially apprehended as the appropriate modulation of desire in such a

5. This position appears in the thought of H. Richard Niebuhr. See especially *The Responsible Self,* and "The Center of Value," in *Radical Monotheism and Western Culture* (New York: Harper and Brothers, 1960), pp. 100–13.

way that motive, intention, and act come to expression in the stable character of the agent. The specific "virtues" which are highlighted in this horizon may vary in their material content. For example, the good person may be viewed as fundamentally characterized by a loving disposition in comparison with the person exhibiting a hostile, hating disposition. Or the good person may be viewed as expressing a fair or just disposition in comparison with those who exhibit an unfair or unjust temperment. Whatever the difference in material content, the locus of virtue is firmly established in the character of the agent.

The fifth and final position articulates a vision of moral experience which is very widespread in modern society. This is the view that apprehends moral experience primarily in terms of the consequences of action for the self and for others. Similar to the horizon which emphasized the notion of responsibility, this view of the moral agent places central value upon the activity of interpretation. It is this activity which brings into view the consequences of moral action, without which there would be no way to measure them in relation to the projects of action. This position generally accepts the necessity of the constant search for energy, but it also brings to attention the destructive consequences of some aspects of nuclear energy. In comparison with the initial position, the ends of action are of acknowledged importance, but the means by which those ends are achieved are evaluated primarily in the light of their consequences in relation to other goods.

Central values which are meaning-compatible in this horizon are the capacities to predict and control consequences. These notions are essential in the experience of freedom which is so characteristic of this value horizon. Freedom means precisely the development of the capacities of prediction and control to such a level that agents will be able to affirm and enact those consequences that are most coherent and supportive of their aims and avoid those consequences that might prove to be destructive or inconsistent with their purposes.

The horizons of value meaning illustrated in this conversation have clearly been conceived as meaning acts of conscious agents. Whether they are routinized, and thus taken for granted, or made explicit during social conflict, they are forms of transcendence which shape the moral sensibilities of individuals in powerful ways. Individuals migrate into these provinces either by routinized or explicit acts, which grant the accent of reality to particular value horizons, or by means of the evocative power of symbols. When such horizons are coexperienced in the social world, then we are involved with a value paradigm that generates a moral tradition which influences the experience of many persons in similar ways.

The analysis has also treated value horizons as meaning-compatible within themselves. Such internal coherence is especially evident during periods of social stability when paradigms of value meaning are deeply sedimented and relatively unquestioned. During periods of social change, however, when experience is pluralized and value paradigms compete in the social world, there is a strain within provinces and meaning-compatibility may be threatened. The uneasiness exhibited in much contemporary moral experience is produced in part because internal meaning-compatibility is weakened and also because there is no reigning paradigm that cuts across the experience of many groups. In this situation moral dissonance is produced by the clash of alternative senses of reality evoked by competing provinces of value meaning.

Although not thematized in a primary way, we should also recall the fact that, because symbols are multivalent, they span more than one province of meaning. Thus the treatment of moral experience in terms of any of the previously discussed horizons might also be extended to a consideration of how value meanings interact, for example, with provinces of religious meaning. A province of value meaning which accented the importance of the ends of action could be related to a religious horizon which emphasized the importance of divine purposes, intentions, and goals. Or a religious horizon that evoked a sense of a divine lawgiver might naturally interact with a horizon of value meaning that emphasizes the centrality of obligation. And in the case of Christianity, a religious province which apprehended Jesus Christ as the exemplar of appropriate moral dispositions would be meaning-compatible with a province of value which viewed the moral life as a life of virtue. Again, during periods of relative social stability, when religious and value horizons may be widely shared, moral and religious experience will be relatively harmonious, although in times of social change there may be severe conflicts among various horizons of meaning.

Horizons of value also intersect with the experience of the everyday world, whatever the conception of its reality may be. The modes of relationship are multiple, but some light may be shed upon this problem by the following examples. When the everyday world appears as essentially harmonious with a province of value meanings, then there is a self-confirmation in experience of that continuity. Or, again, when a province of value meanings is seen to be in tension with a view of the everyday world, then transformations of experience may be forthcoming. In the first case, there is a sense of continuity between the world as it is and the world as it ought to be, whereas in the second instance there is a fissure in experience that renders the everyday world in tension with the image of that world appearing in the light of a value horizon.

ROOT SYMBOLS

What we have done up to this point is describe part of the experiential content which is symbolically mediated by distinguishable horizons of value meaning. The analysis has aimed at showing the different texture, or "tension of consciousness," that is generally evoked by each province.[6] In the light of this argument, moral agency arises as the self apprehends experience in terms of a particular province of value meanings. When the self intends the world in this manner, moral experience is textured in a way that reflects the major motifs that characterize

---

6. In his discussion of the "cognitive style" which characterizes provinces of finite meaning structure, Schutz includes the following elements: a specific form of consciousness, a specific epoche, a particular form of spontaneity, a specific form of self-experience, a particular form of sociality, and a specific time perspective. CP, Vol. I, pp. 230-31; see also SLW, pp. 25-28. Though influenced by Schutz, the treatment in this chapter tends to be more constructive than expository.

the province. The maintenance of a particular sense of moral experience is related directly to the continuing power of the symbols characteristic of the province to mediate a sense of reality. Further analysis of the root symbols illustrated in the initial example will be helpful at this point.

The conversation about nuclear energy showed how root symbols concerning the moral agent tended to order other value meanings in particular ways. In this manner, each horizon achieves a particular experiential shape. For example, the image of the moral agent as fundamentally conditioned by ends highlights some aspects of the moral life as compared with others. Whether the final end is self-realization, happiness, pleasure, or social justice, the importance of purposes, intentions, and projects is central to this view of the moral agent. By comparison, when the root symbol of the moral agent is constituted by the meaning of obligation, then the importance of the conformity of actions to rules, principles, laws, or other action guides will be primary. The importance of purposes and consequences will also be ordered according to this primary symbol. The symbol of responsibility highlights the activity of interpretation as the central modality for assessing the fitting act, and purposes, obligations, or consequences are ordered in the light of this activity. Apprehended under the symbol of virtue, the moral agent is understood in still a different way. Whether viewed in terms of the classical virtues of prudence, temperance, justice, and fortitude or in terms of dispositions to be loving, fair, trustworthy, or sacrificial, moral experience is shaped by a prior order of character. This province of value meaning, whatever its determinate content, accents the goodness of the agent in comparison with the goodness of either ends or obligations. Finally, the importance of consequences as a central symbol apprehends action and experience in its own distinctive manner. Action is good which produces good consequences for agents, whether broadly conceived in terms of the "greatest number" or in terms of more narrowly understood individual goods, such as pleasure.

In a specific cultural order, such as our own, these root symbols may be embodied in persons, such as moral leaders or religious predecessors; or they may be embedded in texts which range from a classical work in ethical theory to a work of art or a drama; or they may be mediated by events which are interpreted so as to highlight their significance. When any one or several of these forms becomes widely shared and deeply sedimented, then the power of the symbolic forms is greatly enhanced. In such situations an encounter with a moral leader, the memory of a religious predecessor embodied in ritual, or reading, seeing, or hearing classical texts, may produce the conditions for migration that were described in the previous chapter. When these conditions are present, then the power of the symbol resides in its capacity to fringe objects, persons, or events with dimensions of transcendent meaning.

Such symbolic vitality produces a deepening moral sensibility which is refracted in and confirmed by the experience of our companions. A sense of other primary experiences, such as the aesthetic and the religious, may reinforce the experience of value, as we have seen. It is also the case that persons, predecessors, texts, and events which form the substance of moral traditions in the social world have lost, to some extent, the capacity to mediate deep value sensibilities. We have suggested that the primary reason for this lies in the dislocation produced when root symbols fail to pair the experience of embodied agents in the everyday world with transcendent value horizons. For many, the experience of the everyday world is either evacuated of transcendent significance or tense with the conflict among competing value horizons. In either case a symbolic hunger is generated which has, up to this time, remained largely unsatisfied by the emergence of a powerful moral tradition.

AGENTIAL GROUNDS OF
MORAL EXPERIENCE

Up to this point it would appear that what we have done is to create a sense of vertigo in experience, especially when we reflect upon the conclusion that, in the modern world, moral experience is likely to be plural in character. Furthermore, we have not made claims concerning the relative adequacy of any particular value province. The primary claim has been that the reality of moral experience emerges as selves image the world according to a horizon of value meanings.

A partial sense of continuity emerges when horizons of value meaning as mediated in individual experience are related to paradigms of value in the social world. But even these wax and wane; they have their history and then are replaced by other paradigms. Another form of continuity emerges when we consider the capacities that enable the self to be capable of multiple levels of experience, one dimension of which is the experience of value. With this reality in view, we can argue that the experience of value is a "natural transcendency," in the sense that selves are embodied creatures with the structural capacities for the experiences of transcendence that we have described.

A more basic explanation is suggested by the analysis, however. We have observed a persistent interpenetration of the horizons of value that have been described. For example, even though moral experience is thematized by a final telos, other elements, such as considerations of obligation, consequences, character, and what is fitting may also be present to some extent. This suggests that each of these value horizons accents an element of agency which is never finally separable from other elements. Thus there is, according to this view, an agential ground that grants a certain legitimacy to each of these renderings of moral experience.

Further exploration of this agential ground will illuminate the interpenetrating character of the horizons of value we have discussed, as well as provide additional evidence for the claim that the capacities of agency described in Chapter I and further elaborated in Chapter II are conditions of possibility for various experiences of value. Experiences of value are meaning acts, as we have shown; what we now focus upon are structures of possibility out of which these meaning acts emerge. In other language, what will be described is the constitutive ground that holds various horizons of value meaning together.

The first horizon of value meaning illustrated by the conversation at the beginning of this chapter had to do with the importance of ends, purposes, or goals for shaping the experiences of moral agents. It is not difficult, given the argument of earlier chapters, to locate the structures which ground this perennial way of apprehending moral experience. They are found precisely in the capacity of human agents to stretch toward a future and, in more complex acts, to image projects which guide behavior. The most general ground of these capacities lies, of course, in the structure of internal time, which was treated in Chapter I.[7]

It is in the very form or nature of human agency that one discovers the roots of the teleological thrust. That this theme recurs in the history of human apprehensions of value is no surprise since it captures a part of the lived experience of moral agents which proceeds from a formal ground that is universal. If value meanings associated with particular end-directed paradigms flavor an entire culture or epoch, the moral experience of many individuals will be so shaped over long historical periods.

The theme of duty as a root symbol mediating a distinctive horizon of value meanings also reflects an aspect of the human being which is essential and not derivative. This primordial reality is our sociality, our essential copresence with others. We apprehend other human beings as a consequence of the pairing described in the first chapter.[8] The experience of the other requires that we respond, even if that response is one of ignoring the other, subordinating the other to a type, or rejecting the other's reality altogether. However the other is apprehended, it is the basic fact of the other's reality which is the anthropological ground for an ethics of duty, no matter how the material content of particular value paradigms may be defined.

For example, the paradigm discussed earlier placed emphasis upon the importance of rules, principles, or law for the regulation of human action. But it is regulation of human action so as properly to embody a structure of mutual obligation and to maintain that structure over time. And as was the case with an emphasis upon ends, a paradigm of value meaning which

7. See pp. 21ff.
8. See pp. 30-31.

thematizes duty may cast its symbolic light over the experience of an entire social group, a culture, or an historical period.

Moral experience which is thematized by the symbol of responsibility cannot, for reasons indicated earlier, exclude the importance of purposes or obligations. The fitting act, however, emerges not as a consequence of obedience or realization of an end, but rather as a consequence of interpretation. The activity of interpretation is grounded in the structure of agency which enables the human being to turn back upon and thus transcend the stream of experience. The apprehension of what is going on is a complex activity which is dependent upon this root capacity, as is the familiar experience of interpreting the meaning of past experience at the autobiographical level. It is also possible to see that moral experience which thematizes consequences as central also emerges from this same ground. At the level of projection, for example, when action is imaged in the future perfect tense, there is the concomitant activity of assessing to what extent imagined projects are realized in the social world. This is an activity of interpretation which highlights consequences, both those that are imagined will occur and those that are retrospectively interpreted as having occurred.

The horizon of value meaning which held character as constitutive of moral experience finds its ground finally in the reality of our embodiment. In Chapter I the theme of embodiment was viewed as an essential aspect of agency. The reality of the body produces an affective ground which energizes our projects.[9] An image of the moral life that emphasizes the importance of rightly shaping desire is grounded in still another aspect of agency which is essential and universal. And this value horizon has also generated moral traditions which have shaped the experience of many individuals and, indeed, entire historical periods.

This explanation of the interpenetration of major value horizons by appeal to the agential structures which ground them has two major consequences. First, it is possible to argue more convincingly that each value horizon will persist in some form

9. See pp. 26ff.

because it is grounded in an essential aspect of agency. But, second, the argument suggests that a constructive view of moral agency and action could be erected upon this understanding. An attempt to outline such a constructive view will be made in Chapter V.

The argument of this chapter can now be summarized and we can anticipate the next step in description. Moral agency and moral experience are species of the generic realities of agency and experience. What qualifies experience and agency as moral is the degree to which agents enter into and grant the accent of reality to a horizon of value meanings. At its highest level, moral agency in the social world involves participation in a moral community which dialectically images a paradigm of value meaning that finds confirmation in the experience of individual agents. And not only is the reality sense of moral experience confirmed but the form in which that experience occurs also is powerfully textured.

Although it was not a primary theme, we also emphasized that value symbols are multivalent, having the capacity to span more than one province of meaning. In a more extended analysis, we would be driven toward a description of how various horizons of value meaning become paired with other primary forms of human transcendence, such as art and religion. If we could understand how value meanings appear in their interrelationship with horizons of aesthetic and religious meaning, then we could grasp something of the flavor which is imparted to historic societies by these basic symbolic forms.

What we must bring into clearer focus in the chapters to follow is the way moral agency is articulated in the social world. Even though the theme of sociality has been introduced as an essential element of the human agent, the nature of the social world and moral communities has not yet clearly been filled out. The task of the next chapter will be to approach this description through a discussion of the moral dimensions of the social world.

IV

Moral Dimensions of the Social World

ONE OF THE FUNDAMENTAL ASPECTS of agency discussed in the first chapter had to do with the theme of social embodiment or sociality. The purpose of this chapter is to fill out the notion of the social world in such a way that its moral dimensions become fully visible. As correlates of symbolic awareness, value meanings find additional grounding in the social world. Social horizons of value meaning arise and persist as a consequence of factors that must receive further elaboration. In order to pursue this task, we will attend to three fundamental dimensions. First, the nature of the social world will be analyzed in a more extensive manner than has been done up to this point. This treatment will gather up parts of the argument that have been alluded to in earlier chapters. The second task will be to locate and describe the temporal dimensions of the social world, which will clarify the problem of the way in which moral traditions are maintained. Finally, the chapter will build toward a vision of the way horizons of value meaning are coexperienced at the level of the social world.

SOCIAL WORLD

In Chapter I we introduced the notion of typification as a capacity of the agent. This feature of consciousness was interpreted as the ground upon which transcendence of a certain sort was made possible. We spoke, for example, of face-to-face communication in which the direct grasp of the other occurred. In such situations, social space is filled with meanings communicated and meanings interpreted. At this level, the reality of experience is constituted by the interpretative grasp of another's meaningful acts. But how are we to have knowledge of others, contemporaries, whose individual or collective action may influence us, but is beyond our reach? Or, again, how are we to have knowledge of predecessors and the traditions which they have formed or anticipate our successors? The answer to these questions lies in the further explication of types and typification. An example will clarify what is meant by types in this context.[1]

A common experience is the meeting, interaction, and parting of friends and acquaintances. If we analyze such experiences closely, we note that communication proceeds at various levels and that our relationship with the other moves from the intimacy of the face-to-face relationship to various forms of typicality. For example, when we disengage the face-to-face relationship, what we have called types fill the social space between us. When you leave, I see you walk away. You may turn and wave, and I respond. But then you are gone and I am alone. Until we meet again, I hold you in memory in typical fashion. Because I have intimate knowledge of you, I am likely to imagine you as engaged in specific activities which I have come to expect of you. We may communicate by letter or telephone, and in this fashion our streams of consciousness may become quasi-simultaneous, but these forms of interaction do not enliven the images we have of each other in the same way as would shared proximity and face-to-face communication. Indeed, when we meet again, the images I have had of you and you of me, the imagined experiences we may have attributed to each other, are expanded, corrected, and shaped by the fresh flow of primary communication.

From this example, it is clear that such personal types are concrete images of another person held in memory or projected in imagination. These types are filled with content derived from the dynamics of previous primary relationships. In distinction from this form of typification, I can hold expectations about the

---

1. Part of the material which follows is based on my article, "The Human Center: Moral Discourse in the Social World," *Journal of Religious Ethics* 5, 2 (1977): 197–208.

activities of others and have experience of them by means of very general, functional types.[2] Such typifying involves "passing by what makes the individual unique and irreplaceable."[3] For example, if I plan to travel by air from one city to another, I may make my first contact by telephone, speaking to a person with whom I have had no direct experience. I typify this person under the rubric of "reservation clerk." I also depend upon a series of activities performed by many others who occupy general, functional roles in relation to me. I assume that "bank personnel" will honor my check and the "postal employees" will deliver my tickets by mail. On the day of my flight, I depend upon the coordinated activity of anonymous others whose roles are important to me but with whom I normally will have no personal relationship: taxi drivers, baggage clerks, maintenance crews, pilots, and so on. I may have a general understanding of what these persons do in relation to my travel plans, but usually my notions are vague and I give them little thought. Until a crisis interrupts my expectations, I proceed in a routine manner.

From this example we can see that typification is not only characteristic of all social relationships but also absolutely essential for experiencing others beyond an intimate interaction. In this way I can orient my action to the action of my contemporaries and, through typification, bring a portion of the social world into reach. Through bodily movements and, in this case, acts of communication, I can gear into the social world. I "know" how to do this through previous experience, the initial phases of which I usually receive from my social companions.[4] This social stock of knowledge is a structure of typifications which makes such practical activities as we have described possible. Even in the primary relations dealt with above, typifications are operative at a general level, since these relations presuppose a stock of knowledge which includes linguistic recipes, routinized understandings of meanings embodied in gestures, facial expressions, and so on.

Typification is also the fundamental mode of relating to in-

2. Alfred Schutz, SLW, pp. 82 ff.
3. Schutz, CP, Vol. II, p. 234.
4. Schutz, SLW, pp. 66 ff.

stitutional entities in the social world such as the Congress, the Central Intelligence Agency, or the Yale Corporation. I assume that it is possible to establish a primary relationship with one of the members of such abstract collectivities, but normally I do not. But I bring both individuals and the entities they represent into my experience by typifying them and their functions in relation to me. Beyond such relations are essentially anonymous entities with which no personal relationship is possible: a particular economic system, the rules of grammar in a specific language, or the artifacts of a past civilization which refer to meaning contexts and actors who originated them but who are no longer available to my direct experience.[5]

It is also through typification that we are able to relate to the world of predecessors. Here it is necessary to recall a fundamental distinction in order to indicate a critical difference among predecessors.[6] The distinction is between predecessors with whom I have had previous personal experience and those who are my former contemporaries but with whom I have had no face-to-face relationship. In the first case, the predecessor is available to present experience in typical ways, and these types are filled in by acts of imagination. Such acts of recollection and imagination are based upon my own sedimented experience. Here we are dealing with personal types in the memorial mode, though they have to do not with contemporaries with whom we can relate again, but rather with a predecessor with whom we once related but whose world and subjective reality is forever beyond reach—except in the memorial mode.

In the second case there are predecessors with whom I have had no personal relationship. These predecessors are related to me and I bring them into my experience by means of types which receive their content from loci other than my personal experience. In the case of political or religious predecessors, for example, I may fill in typifications concerning their identity and activity through reading their writings or entering into a tradition of interpretation concerning their meaning. However I fill

5. Ibid., pp. 82–84.
6. I have analyzed this problem in "Christ as Predecessor and Contemporary," *Journal of the American Academy of Religion* 44, 2 (1976): 289–97.

in the types, and from whatever sources, such filling in essentially involves acts of imagination which construct a past that transcends personal experience but at the same time can be shared with others.

Finally, it is through types alone that we can anticipate a world populated by our successors. In this case, however, the types are relatively empty. We know that we will join the world of predecessors and that others will come after us. We may project onto these successors concrete personality traits, and in the case of familial relationships such types may approach concreteness through the play of imagination as we project the identity of our "grandchildren" or our "great grandchildren." For the most part, however, this host of imagined others are anonymous precursors of a social world that we may expect and anticipate but which is radically beyond our reach in comparison with typical reconstructions of the past.[7]

In its deepest sense, what is implied in the foregoing analysis is that the social world is, at one level of experience, a structure of types. What we call institutions, such as the family, the state, and so on, are not external realities in the physical sense. They are rather unities of meaning, the possibility of which is given in the capacity to transcend experience through typification. These unities of meaning, which express every major human activity, *are* institutions.[8] They are maintained in experience by being widely shared, and they are changed by changing the meanings which are borne in the linguistic, attitudinal, and affective dimensions of the experience of individuals. In a basic sense, then, changes in the social world are changes in the unities of meaning, the institutions, of which that world is composed. The level upon which this understanding of institutions arises is the human capacity to typify; it is the exercise of this capacity that constitutes large portions of the taken-for-granted everyday world.

The taken-for-granted world, which is the social a priori of all

7. Schutz, SLW, pp. 87–92.
8. This point of view is dependent upon the analysis of Maurice Natanson in *Phenomenology, Role and Reason* (Springfield, Ill.: Charles C Thomas, 1974), pp. 132, 133–36.

our actions and interpretations, is available to us not only through the operation of types by which we transcend present experience; there is also the migration that we described earlier which is accomplished through the medium of symbols. We can elaborate this understanding by extending our example of the way we relate to various sorts of predecessors. As we have seen, it is possible to relate to predecessors with whom we have had a previous personal relationship by means of types that become the objects of various acts of recollection. But we also have experiences in which memory is activated and "rises up" without our actively typifying experience in acts of recollection. Such entries into worlds of memorial meaning may be activated by objects, events, or actions that perform a symbolic function in experience, evoking a world of meaning in a powerful and often surprising manner. For example, one of our significant predecessors may have had the habit of carving wood.[9] If we have the predecessor's knife in our possession, then it may become for us a special object, invested with the significance of the one who once used it. When we see the knife it can perform a symbolic function in experience; because it is paired with memories of the predecessor, it may evoke in experience reveries that rise up without our active attention.

In the case of the knife, that which becomes a symbol is quite specifically related to my biographical situation. It may be that other family members have shared experiences with me in such a way that the same artifact could perform for them a similar symbolic function. It is doubtful that anyone beyond the family would see anything but a knife of a certain shape and size. Its functions as a knife would be grasped typically, of course. But the world of memorial meanings which the knife can symbolically activate in my experience and perhaps in the experience of family members is closed to others—unless they come to share in the story of the predecessor. In this case, the symbol may be shared more widely.

If we move to consider predecessors in political communities, then in addition to types that are filled with interpretative con-

9. Part of the material that follows is based upon my article, "Christ as Predecessor and Contemporary," p. 296.

tent, there are also complex symbols that can evoke in experience particular worlds of memorial meaning. For instance, the flag is a material object of a certain shape and color. As flag, we apprehend its meaning in a typical fashion at the level of referential meaning. But as *flag* it is also invested with the transcendent significance of the republic for which it stands. An individual who sees the flag may have evoked in experience something of the memorial tradition of the republic—anything from an imaginary conversation with Abraham Lincoln, to an understanding of the sacrifice and moral significance of World War II, to a vague sense of sentimental warmth concerning "my country."

The flag is also a shared symbol which can orient corporate attention and experience to what are believed to be the significant meanings of the republic. For example, Memorial Day is an occasion when the flag can activate the memory of a brother or father killed in battle, as well as the more anonymous memory of all our "honored dead." The specialized meaning which the flag may have for an individual will vary widely according to personal biography; but at the corporate level there is also shared meaning. Even though the worlds of meaning vary and range from concrete personal memory to highly anonymous meanings, the flag as multivalent symbol can activate them all.

It is important to emphasize once again that the typification of others, objects, and events is a necessary layer in experience in relation to which symbols arise and evoke their worlds of meaning. That which is typical in experience at one time, or for some individuals and groups, may be symbolic for other individuals and groups; and that which has been symbolic may again become typical. For example, an anonymous role such as "postman" may become symbolic when it appears in a world of dramatic meaning. Likewise, the opposite is true, and the world of meaning which was once evoked by symbols fades from view and assumes a typical form in experience.

From this perspective, the social world arises and attains its intersubjective reality as a consequence of mutual typical and symbolic meaning structures. The importance of this view for the analysis of value meanings can now be extended further. In the first place, it ought to be clearer how the experience of value appears within the context of the dimensions of the social world that have been outlined. For instance, the matrix of communication within the face-to-face context is the locus where primary meanings, including those relating to value experiences, are communicated. Such communication depends upon the operation of deeply shared typifications concerning the definition of the human, the social, and the natural contexts. When imbedded in a common language, these typifications expand into a circle of shared understanding and coexperienced meaning. We receive a sense of what is appropriate, what is right, and what is fitting from important others; and these meanings also appear as a part of the shared reality which is a common social world.

Second, when we move from face-to-face relations into the realm of contemporaries who are experienced under types, then the value meanings that are a dimension of autobiography become reinforced by or in conflict with these more anonymous levels of the social world. For example, the social roles of teacher, law enforcement officer, and government official may bring to experience values associated with the legitimacy of the educational process, the appropriateness of social order, or the values to which the life of politics bears witness. In a *society* it is imperative that meanings typified in social roles such as these be reflected at the experiential level by the individuals who compose various subgroups. If such levels of shared meaning begin to break down, then the basic cohesion of the group is threatened and various sorts of social change may be induced as individuals and groups seek to retypify the social world. This problem will be addressed at greater length in the last chapter, where we take up the issue of moral discourse.

Third, the analysis of predecessors who are temporally separated from contemporary experience brought into view the symbolic dimension of the social world. Predecessors who are separated from our experience by the intervention of many generations, and who perform a symbolic function, are often viewed as the originators of moral traditions. The meaning of these predecessors is likely to be a multilayered reality, resulting from the process of continual interpretation and reinterpretation by each succeeding generation.

Examples of significant predecessors who are separated by different time frames are found in the figures of Gandhi and Jesus Christ. When interpreted by a third figure, Martin Luther King, these predecessors evoked a horizon of transcendent meaning structure that ordered the action and interpretation of a social movement. Gandhi evoked a vision of political action which was based upon a particular understanding of love. This love was active, resistant of evil, politically astute, but nonviolent. When interpreted by King, the love represented in Jesus Christ by some interpreters as apolitical, became transformed into a principle of nonviolent social action that funded the civil rights movement with a powerful horizon of value meanings.

The aspects of the social world that have been analyzed depend upon structures and processes that must receive further explication. We are now able to understand some of the ways in which meanings arising from the experience of human agents become shared realities. What is not entirely clear is how these levels of typical and symbolic meaning structure are maintained intersubjectively and how they are potentially available as horizons which may rise up or be liturgically evoked in the experience of many individuals. In order to clarify these problems, we must turn to a consideration of the social grounds for what has been analyzed under the rubrics of internal time consciousness and multiple levels of experience. The moral dimensions of the social world are dependent for their continued sense of reality upon social time and provinces of value meaning that are intersubjectively experienced.

SOCIAL TIME

Structures enabling the grasp of each past phase of experience and the capacity to stretch forward in anticipation were interpreted as grounds for memory and imaging a future, both of which were viewed as constitutions within internal time. Even though the social world has been interpreted as originating in an "immanent fiat"[10] of consciousness which is intersubjectively maintained, the social world does not possess the qualities of in-

10. The term is Natanson's. Ibid. See *Phenomenology, Role and Reason.*

81

dividual consciousness. That is, even though the social world is an intersubjective emergent, there is no such thing as a "social mind." The correlates of memory and projection in the social world are analogous in function but not identical in form to those that pertain to individual agents.[11] When we speak of social past and social future, the realities to which we refer are dependent upon the continual intersubjective intending of a social world by individual agents; the realities of the social world arise as meaning structures which are dialectically related to the noetic acts that produce them. But at another level it is possible to isolate and describe functional equivalents in the social world that constitute the possibility for experiencing a social past and anticipating a social future.

At a concrete level, the social past is the coexperienced story of predecessors and their larger social meaning; and the social future is the image of shared projects which we, along with our contemporaries, hope to realize. What are the social processes that make possible the unity and continuity of the social world as it appears in the form of a shared temporality? If these problems can be illuminated, then we will have greater understanding of the general matrix which conditions the formation of moral traditions and moral projects.

This issue is important precisely because we have to give an account of how traditions of interpretation are at hand for understanding societal identity at any given point and how visions of societal destiny arise to lure a social group into a determinate future. Three dimensions will be discussed which bear directly upon this analysis. The first dimension has to do with principles by which meanings of any sort are sedimented in the social world; second, there is the complex problem of social memory and projection; and, third, there are modes of transmission and preservation that hold certain meaning horizons in place so that they are potentially or actually available to the experience of individuals who compose a social group.

Before description proceeds, it is well to recall once again that meanings arise as a consequence of intentional acts and are, at

11. Schutz, SLW, pp. 262 ff.

the biographical level, articulated as horizons within inner time. What we are seeking to unravel at this juncture involves the way in which the multiple horizons of awareness that characterize human experience are transmuted into horizons that are coexperienced in such a manner that a larger center of luminosity arises—the social world. The dialectic through which meanings become shared is the final focus; the more immediate task is to describe conditions of possibility for the sedimentation of meanings in the social world.

The first principle that conditions *what* meanings will be sedimented has to do with the social relevance of certain meaning horizons. Examples will assist reflection at this juncture and will serve to illustrate this very complex but important problem. For instance, among several Native American tribes living on the great plains during the nineteenth century there was a deep dependence upon the horse and the buffalo. A study of these plains groups reveals extensive structures of typified knowledge concerning these two animals. This knowledge was preserved in recipe fashion and passed systematically from one generation to the next. Men knew, for example, what the varieties of grasses were and where the best grazing land for horses could be located; considerable knowledge of horse breeding was available; and knowledge of how to treat diseases which afflicted horses was typically present. Likewise, both men and women knew how to preserve meat from the buffalo and how to make use of almost all of the flesh, bone, and skin of this great mammal.[12]

The obvious point to be derived from this example is that knowledge concerning horses and buffalo was routinely sedimented and typically available *because* it was relevant for the continued existence of the group. In contemporary society, typical structures of knowledge concerning butchering and preserving meat have disappeared from the experience of a large

---

12. See, for example, John C. Ewers, "The Horse in Blackfoot Indian Culture," *Bureau of American Ethnology Bulletin 159* (Washington, D.C.: U.S. Government Printing Office, 1955), pp. 40–41, 46–50, 53–58; and Ewers, *The Blackfeet* (Norman: Oklahoma University Press, 1958), ch. 4.

number of people. In a society in which the consumption of prepared and processed foods assumes a dominant modality, the social relevance of systems of knowledge concerning the private preparation of food and its preservation declines in importance and such knowledge may disappear altogether. At the level of empirical knowledge, what is sedimented and preserved in the stock of typical knowledge is dependent upon its perceived relevance. And it is clear that perceived relevance may change over time, which means that the social stock of knowledge is a complex structure of shared meanings possessing open and moving horizons.

Perceived relevance of empirical systems of knowledge may be radically influenced by actual or potential threats to the social group. A convenient illustration of this point is the threat posed to the United States by the Russian success in putting sputnik into orbit in 1957. This event was interpreted by political leaders as a serious challenge to national security; and sufficient typical and symbolic agreement was amassed to initiate widespread changes in the way children were trained in mathematics and basic science. This social project gradually produced a generation of persons who, it was believed, could meet the scientific and technical challenges produced by the competition between the United States and the Soviet Union. The symbol of the "space age" describes an emergent paradigm which came to organize the experience and action of many individuals.

The principles that apply to an understanding of knowledge which is sedimented in order to deal with so-called "empirical" matters can be extended to other sorts of meaning structures. For example, among the plains tribes during the nineteenth century there was both empirical knowledge, illustrated earlier, and ritual knowledge which was typically preserved and transmitted across generational time. This ritual knowledge was the carrier of provinces of religious and moral meanings which survived continual assaults by various representatives of an increasingly dominant white culture. These distinctive religious and moral meanings were clearly perceived as relevant to the continuing existence of the group; and among those who ceased to share this assumption, provinces of religious and moral meaning that characterized an earlier generation gradually faded from view, perhaps to be replaced by the sedimentation of meaning structures from other religious and moral traditions.[13] Examples of moral values which were mediated in one tribe as a part of an intersubjectively experienced horizon of value meanings were the virtues of generosity and bravery, which defined the male identity, and chastity, which defined the quality of life women ought to embody.[14] The definition of appropriate identity patterns for men and women was ritually reinforced and given further support by horizons of religious significance that became paired with provinces of value meaning.

Sedimentation of empirical knowledge, ritual meanings, moral traditions, as well as other horizons of social meaning structure is not only governed by relevance but also receives its structure in a certain manner. In the experience of individuals, sedimentation is ordered by the affinity of each experiential duration with the province of meaning out of which it arises. In other words, dreams, fantasies, religious experiences, memories, value sensibilities, and practical activities are typically sedimented according to the province of meaning with which they were originally associated. This is also the case with coexperienced meanings forming the fabric of the social world.[15] Thus in ordinary communication, adult members of a society normally do not confuse a discussion of dreams or fantasies

13. It was often the case that items from religious traditions represented by Protestant and Catholic missionaries were taken over by Native Americans in a quite selective manner. This fact makes it exceedingly difficult to make a clear judgment about how complete the process of religious acculturation really was during the nineteenth and early twentieth centuries.

14. For male virtues, see George Bird Grinnell, *Blackfoot Lodge Tales* (New York: Charles Scribners, 1892), p. 219; Clark Wissler, "Social Organization and Ritualistic Ceremonies of the Blackfoot Indians," *Anthropological Papers of the American Museum of Natural History* VII (1912), p. 23; and Ewers, "The Horse," p. 246. For a description of how harsh the punishment for female violations of the virtue of chastity was, see Alexander Philip Maximilian (Prince of Weid Neuweid), *Travels in the Interior of North America,* trans. H. Evans Lloyd (London: Ackerman and Company, 1843), pp. 256–57.

15. Schutz, SLW, pp. 122–223.

with a practical project. Of course, the way such experience is sedimented and forms the contours of the social world is imposed upon each new generation if the society continues to exist in its traditional form. Preformed sedimentations concerning the differences between dreams, fantasies, religious experience, and so on will be imposed upon children. If this social process is successful, then children will develop routine associations with the taken-for-granted order among the provinces of meaning which characterize the group.

Turning now from the general principles that govern how sedimentation occurs, we come to the second dimension which explains how a sense of the social past is constituted. Part of the social past are moral traditions, but these traditions are sedimented and made available by the operation of a social memory which invites further, more general, description. We have seen how it is possible for an individual to turn back upon elapsed experience in acts of recollection, acts which grant the accent of reality to worlds of memorial meaning. These meanings are directly available for recovery and reconstitution because the locus of experience is autobiographical. Meanings which form the horizons of memorial experience are meanings constituted by acts of interpretation by the same self who turns back in acts of recollection and who lived through the experience in the first place. The social past is constituted differently from the biographical past. There are similarities, of course, such as the fact that the meanings forming horizons of the social world and those that fill biography are both products of human agency. At this juncture, an example will perhaps help to clarify both the similarities and the differences between these two levels of experience.

For the generation living through the period 1929–1932, the complex meaning structure known as the Great Depression was a matter of biographical experience. For that generation, experience was typified in such a manner that it became widely shared. Of course, the typification of experience varied among groups so that the overall meaning of the Great Depression was different for the small farmer in the midwest, for the unemployed worker in the urban center, and for the owner of stocks on Wall Street. Despite these important variations, for the generation that endured the Great Depression, recollection is characterized by a return to meaning horizons that are both biographically specific and typically shared by the group with which the remembering individual is associated.[16] From the point of view of the present, the Great Depression remains a meaning structure sedimented in the experience of contemporaries, those persons still alive whose experience of 1929–1932 is the subject of primary memory. It is also a meaning structure which is borne in the cumulative interpretations of predecessors who typified the meaning of the Great Depression in more complex hermeneutical acts. Examples of such acts of interpretation are found in the accounts of historians, commentators, and novelists. At another level, the portrayal of the meaning of the Great Depression in aesthetic provinces of meaning was accomplished by artists and creators of folk music.

These interpreters constitute the meaning of the social past as a horizon which is available for appropriation by individuals. It is a past that is typically and symbolically embodied in story, narrative, and art form. Even though it has not been experienced personally, it is still possible for such a past to be widely shared if the cultural texts which embody significant meaning structures evoke a sense of their reality. This occurs, as we have argued, when types and symbols bearing the meaning of the social past are widely shared and granted the accent of reality. When celebrated liturgically in a community, the social past arises as a powerful reality dialectically related to the depths of biographical sensibilities concerning the past.

Another important layer of meaning associated with the experience of the Great Depression involves values. For instance, thrift and conservation were virtues, and many individuals developed a healthy suspicion of money as a stable value; this latter theme led to an emphasis on land as a source of value. It is interesting to observe that an appeal is being made to meaning horizons which mediate a sensibility concerning these virtues by political leaders who are presently seeking to deal with world-

---

16. For an analysis of the way generational experience is constituted and mediated, see Karl Mannheim, *Essays on the Sociology of Knowledge*, ed. Paul Kecskemeti (London: Routledge & Kegan Paul, 1952), ch. VII.

wide crises produced by diminishing resources. For those whose memory is conditioned by primary experience during the Great Depression, the symbols articulated by political leaders may find resonance at the experiential level. By contrast, for those whose experience is conditioned by a sense of unlimited growth and material abundance, the appeal to a horizon of value meaning which has affinity with the Great Depression may seem alien and lacking in experiential power. It could be argued that the experience of many individuals presently is characterized by a conflict between these two horizons of value meaning.

We have now uncovered dimensions of the social world that enable individuals to share a sense of a common past. Horizons of meaning that constitute the social past are not without their ambiguity, and in times of social crisis a process of reinterpretation may arise in an attempt to recover a stable sense of social identity. It is also possible for a sense of the social future to arise and to become embodied in projects that are viewed as consistent with social identity.

The envisioning of a concrete social future in the form of specific projects is dependent upon the interpretative and projective activity of individuals, many of whom play powerful social roles; social projects are also envisioned and maintained through the activity of elites or interpreting communities. The imagining of a social future may take several forms. For example, the envisioning of societal destiny may take the form of a recovery of a past tradition or traditions; those who occupy key interpreting roles will view such projection as a recovery of authenticity or as an affirmation of continuity with the past. Or the vision of a social future may emerge out of a process not of recovery, but rather of reinterpretation of what are believed to be the normative traditions of the group.

Reinterpretation may be more or less radical, but the images that emerge from such a process are often believed to represent the original intention of the founding predecessors. Or the vision of the future may arise out of a social process that ends in what is believed to be a discovery of an alternative tradition, which then becomes the substance of the group's interpretative horizon. Or, finally, the process of social projection may be presented in a form that appeals to radical innovation. Such claims view the anticipated direction of the societal future in terms of a destiny that is discontinuous with the past. If this is actually the case, then we are in the presence of the origination of new traditions, horizons of meaning which have not been present as a part of the social world.

Conflict in the social world can be viewed, at one level, as a conflict between meaning structures that provide alternative interpretations of the past and projections about the future. The resolution, or social choice, among competing and conflicting projects in the social world occurs when the meanings mediated through types and symbols become relatively consistent in the experience of a dominant number of individuals. One of the characteristics of modern societies is that major meaning conflicts which deal with societal destiny are often protracted, and even if a dominant meaning structure emerges, the resolution is uneasy because there are smaller groups who continue to hold quite different senses of the future. Modern societies are often characterized by a major theme that states a fundamental direction but is unable completely to mute the cacophony of dissident meaning structures.

A convenient example which illustrates the argument at this juncture is the relation between blacks and the white majority in the United States. In the distant and even the more recent past, alternative projects for dealing with the relation between these two groups have been debated at the level of public policy. Whether the project was framed in terms of an assimilative, an integrationist, or a secessionist model, each way of framing the solution was a representation of certain value horizons. The meanings of key value terms, such as equality and justice, were experienced in ways that varied greatly among subgroups. Each of these projects and their horizons of value meaning represented a possibility that could become a dominant theme for organizing relations between the two groups. That no theme has become completely dominant is the reason why the social instability that characterizes this problem continues.[17]

---

17. On the issue of pluralism in experience at the point of values, see Alfred Schutz, "Equality and the Meaning Structure of the Social World," CP, Vol. II, pp. 226-74.

Each of the projects mentioned above carried with it a different interpretation of the nation's past: America is a melting pot, assimilating all differences within a common culture; America is a pluralistic culture which can tolerate the presence of diverse and often conflicting cultures; or America is, from the point of view of the black minority, a culture from which one withdraws. None of these images of societal identity has become completely dominant for either group. Intellectual elites, such as revisionist historians, civil rights groups, and political groups have, along with others, sought to render an adequate interpretation. But conflicts of value continue, and the emergence of societal identity and common projects concerning this problem remains a future possibility rather than a present reality.

Societal projects and interpretations of identity have also emerged around such issues as the status and future of Native Americans, the proper conduct of national defense, the problems of economic justice and poverty in America, and, more recently, concerns with health care and energy. All of these issues have been or presently are the subject of interpretation in terms of societal identity and projection. Individual agents who participate in the conflict of interpretations and competing possibilities at the level of the social world may find themselves reflecting in their own experience the ambiguities and value conflicts deriving from the clash of alternative social paradigms.

During times of partial resolution there is an emerging sense of integrity. For example, during the civil rights movement there were times when some individuals felt an emerging coherence among interpretation, project, horizon of value, and action. Such was also the case during the War on Poverty and discussions of the Vietnam War. But these resolutions were short-lived, and the present social world is characterized more by confusion of societal identity and inability to choose a dominant project. These themes are reflected in moral confusion and paralysis at the level of individual action.

We will bring this discussion of the temporal dimensions of the social world to a close by briefly considering the problem of transmission and preservation of socially constructed meaning structures. Sedimentation in artifact, story, history, and myth are modalities by which the meanings of predecessors and past events are sustained and made potentially available to present experience. It is the act of interpretative entry into these past meaning horizons which fills them with present luminosity. For example, the arc of meaning which is a consequence of imaginal entry into the written story of a significant predecessor suffuses present experience with a sense of continuity with the past. When this arc of meaning is widely shared, and when the same text, artifact, or story evokes similar meanings in the experience of individuals, then the luminous center expands into a sense of common past. When this happens, what was sedimented by interpreting the activity of predecessors becomes a horizon of meaning which is coexperienced by a group.

At this point the question arises concerning the way in which particular interpretations of a social past or visions of a social future are authorized. In smaller, less complex societies, as well as in larger complex societies, there are social roles and social groups that struggle to authorize a reigning interpretation of the group's past. In periods of relative stability, such social interpretations may be without significant conflict, whereas in times of social crisis a conflict of interpretations usually arises.

Tribal societies, for example, normally preserve a sense of the past by means of an oral tradition, generationally transmitted, and rehearsed in complex social rituals. In addition, there is an interdependent system of social roles, such as elders, political leaders, religious elites, and so on, which function as mediators and interpreters of societal identity and destiny. Out of the interaction of these various social roles emerges a sense of meaning that is typically and symbolically shared by the group. In complex modern societies, by contrast, the sense of the past is preserved and mediated by means of a combination of oral and written communication. Entire institutional contexts, such as schools, are responsible for maintaining and reinterpreting the social past. In addition, there are social roles, such as the political and the religious, which contribute to the process of constituting a sense of the social past. In both the small and the more complex society, the outcome of all of these social processes is the emergence of a public interpretation of reality that is more or less shared by the members of a group.[18]

Interpreted meanings which are sedimented, shared, and transmitted through institutions and social roles form the determinate horizons of a social past. In a way that is analogous to the individual, the sense of a social past can be precarious, and its horizons may contain open dimensions of possibility. Even though precarious and subject to change and reinterpretation, this sense of the past is the source of societal continuity and identity. It is maintained by complex social acts, and it is mirrored in the interpretations of those who coexperience it. This reservoir of sedimented meanings is the touchstone for the construction of visions of a social future and a measure for indicating whether tendencies of present experience conform to or conflict with interpretations of societal identity and destiny.

PARADIGMS OF VALUE MEANING

It is now possible to gather up and make more systematic the view of paradigms of value meaning as these function at the level of individual experience and in the social world. A paradigm of value meaning has been interpreted as a structure which is sedimented in texts, both written and oral, is mediated and preserved in social roles and social groups, and is represented and revivified in various sorts of ritual processes. Here a paradigm of value meaning appears in the form of a moral tradition. Paradigms of value meaning were also interpreted as sources of experiential reality, and the formal condition for entering into any given province of value meaning lies in the continuing power of the symbols to bear its reality to the experience of individuals.

Whatever their determinate content, provinces of value meaning function at the agential level as horizons which order the activities of interpretation and projection. When the accent of reality is granted at an intersubjective level, then paradigms of value meaning have the power to order interpretation and

---

18. Schutz, CP, Vol. I, p. 348.

projection in a larger social group. Concrete relations between self and others, appropriate relations among groups, the values that are understood to ground individual and group identity, and the strivings that are seen to be legitimate images of the future are all ordered by provinces of value meaning with determinate social and experiential content.

The argument that has been developed in this chapter has dealt mainly with the formal elements which must be understood in order to have a clear view of moral dimensions of the social world. Upon first glance, it may seem that discussions of modes of social duration, which have formed a large part of the analysis, are not clearly related to what we have called "moral dimensions" of the social world. Further reflection shows, however, that the achievement of societal identity and envisioning of societal destiny are activities that are essentially conditioned by horizons of value meaning. The conditions in the social world which make interpretation and projection possible are thus "moral dimensions" in a very concrete sense.

We have surveyed some of the structures and processes which are conditions of possibility for the emergence of social time, and we have connected these elements to an understanding of how moral traditions arise and are maintained. The purpose of the next chapter is to explicate in greater detail the way moral agency expresses itself in the social world. This analysis will lead toward a description of the processes of deliberation and choice seen from the perspective of both the agent and the social world. When this analysis is complete, we will return once more to a theme which has appeared again and again in the course of these chapters. This is the theme of social change and the place of moral discourse in the process of change. An analysis of this problem will form the subject matter for the final chapter on moral discourse in the social world.

V

Moral Agency in the
Social World

THE UNDERSTANDING OF AGENCY, a view of how the self experiences value, a description of how moral experience occurs, and a view of the moral dimensions of the social world have provided elements which build toward an image of the self engaging in choice and action. Two previously introduced themes will be interpreted as essential ingredients in this developing understanding of the self as moral agent in the social world.

The first element is interpretation, that activity through which the agent discerns patterns of significance, whether in relation to personal history or in the larger social world. The activity of interpretation will be viewed as that process through which the self achieves a sense of identity and integrity. The second element is projection, which will be understood as that activity of the self which provides the conditions of possibility for deliberation and choice. In this case an act of future-directed imagination is involved in the portrayal of differing possibilities for action. It is the oscillation among possible courses of action which characterizes the self in the deliberative mode. The emergence of a dominant project gathers up the sense of identity that has emerged from retrospective interpreting and moves the self toward a vision of appropriate actions and relations with others. Choice is an act of closure which stops deliberation and impels projects into the social world where they become sources of innovation and social change.

The basic distinction, also introduced earlier, between

routinized and fully self-conscious action will give additional form to the analysis. This distinction points toward a continuum running throughout all experience, and in all of its action the self articulates itself in a dominant manner at some point along this continuum. In many of its actions the self is responsive in a routine manner and action proceeds without the self taking thought. It is when taken-for-granted recipes for action begin to break down that an emerging crisis in experience occurs, forcing the self to attend to its action in a more self-conscious manner. However, the self in all of its action is never at a single place on the continuum between routinization and self-consciousness. These dimensions interpenetrate each other in actual experience so that some phases of action may proceed in a routine manner while other phases may become objects of self-conscious reflection. For example, we may be able to engage in concrete acts, such as walking or working, while at another level of consciousness we are grappling with a problem that has broken through our taken-for-granted formulas for its solution. The image of the continuum is not meant to describe points upon which action can be located absolutely; rather, it is a heuristic device that illuminates a dynamically interpenetrating process.

Action that is ordered by routine acts of interpretation and projection is based upon deeply shared and unquestioned horizons of value meaning. During periods of social change, individual and societal identity and destiny are no longer matters of recipe knowledge, but emerge as problematic. Horizons of value meaning which were once unquestioned lose their reality sense and their symbols no longer have the power to evoke moral experience. It is in response to this problematic character of moral experience that struggle emerges and interpretation and projection become self-conscious activities. When we take up the question of moral discourse in the next chapter, we will learn that interpretation and projection involve the search for a horizon of value which is adequate to the self's emerging sense of identity and integrity. This analysis ought to illuminate contemporary experiences, many of which are concerned precisely with a breakdown of shared meaning horizons and the emergence of crises both at the individual level and in the social world. The attempt will be to discern at a greater level of depth what is going on in such experiences rather than to provide a single constructive solution to the problem.

ROUTINIZED INTERPRETATION AND PROJECTION

The analysis unfolded in the previous chapters can illuminate our understanding of the taken-for-granted world as a value-laden reality within which routinized action by moral agents takes place. Such routinized action is oriented at one level by means of typical understandings of major social roles, such as soldier, husband, father, mother, doctor, priest, and so on. Such sedimented typifications are the product of the actions and interpretations of predecessors. The form in which they come to present experience is in the structure of typifications, present in a primordial form in our language, by which we understand and apprehend the meanings associated with social roles. These meanings have to do not only with descriptive images about motivated role performance, for example, that a father works at a job in order to support his family. They are also related to other horizons of meaning which are signaled by such expressions as, "A father (or mother) *ought* to work in order to support his (or her) family." This normative level is related to horizons of value meaning that are more or less coherent and that are evoked symbolically in experience. As long as we remain on the level of taken-for-granted morality, action and interpretation unfold routinely in relation both to structures of typification constituting the social roles and to levels of value meaning evoked routinely by symbols. Acts of memory and projection within the stream of consciousness fill in the experience of the agent in such a way that there is relative conformity between the descriptive–typical and the normative–symbolic elements of experience; and these, in turn, are related to typical and symbolic sedimentations in the social world.

The identity of the self is constituted in such a way that the interpretation of what is appropriate to the social role of father, for example, is "at hand" and is activated in experience without the need to "take thought." Likewise, the experiences of value that infuse the descriptive significance of the role with normative elements are also dependent upon a process that is activated by symbols operating at a taken-for-granted level.

Imposed themes are present in the pregiven typifications and symbols surrounding social roles. These imposed themes become motives for individuals and are sedimented in their biographical stock of knowledge. By the time a male child has become an adult, for example, the typical and symbolic meanings surrounding the social roles of father may be sedimented as part of personal history and identity. At the point in personal life when the social project of constituting a family and becoming a father comes into view, the foundations for the personal project of getting married and having children has become a taken-for-granted meaning structure orienting the agent's action. The typical sequences of action which are necessary to realize the project are fantasized in the future perfect tense; and when the act is completed in the social world, it is retained in memorial experience as a significant personal event which becomes the subject of various acts of recollection and interpretation and may, under certain circumstances, become a symbolic vehicle in experience. The context within which interpretation and reinterpretation proceed includes not only typical understandings at the level of law and the broader social system; there are also important normative elements that derive from the symbolic mediation of value meanings in experience. How these value meanings are organized and what their content is will depend upon the nature of the province of value.

What is meant when we say that the social world is value-laden should now be clearer. All major roles in a given society relate to significant social projects and are, from the point of view we are developing, structures of meaning which are more or less coherently related. They are also related to horizons of value meaning that are more or less well organized. As long as relative coherence at these two levels is maintained, we can speak accurately of a social group in the sense of an intersubjective sharing of meanings and projects. Each major network of meaning surrounding social roles and projects is related to a horizon of value meanings that gives it experiential significance at a deeper level. These horizons of value meaning, when they are widely shared, are normative paradigms in the light of which the experience of individuals in the particular social group is interpreted.

In any concrete society, paradigms of value meaning do not comprehend all of the variations that are present, of course. This is especially the case in large, complex societies. Underneath the reigning value paradigm, which provides a horizon of significance for concrete social roles, there may exist competing and often conflicting horizons of value meaning. These are evoked symbolically in the experience of such groups as ethnic minorities and religious or cultural minorities. In such cases, major social roles are typified and symbolically mediated in a manner that is significantly different within different groups. The dominant group will more than likely continue to experience its paradigm as the fundamental reality; but at the edges of awareness there is often the intrusion of alien paradigms.

During periods of social change, which at its deepest level represents shifts in basic meaning structures, there may appear a lack of congruity between major social projects, social roles, and the way these are apprehended in experience. Such a period in recent American history was the Vietnam War, during which basic changes took place in the understanding of the nation's political role, and fundamental institutions, such as the draft, were changed. Other basic changes are unfolding at present, such as those pertaining to understandings of the relationship between men and women in the institution of the family. Shifts in meaning and evaluation are grasped interpretatively, and an attempt is made to relate emerging meanings to previously sedimented experience. As meanings continue to diverge, however, the process of routine interpretation is upset and an area of self-experience becomes increasingly problematic. Disturbances are perhaps most painful for the self as the horizon of value meanings motivating action in a routine manner begins to lose its power. A conflict of interpretation ensues in which the self seeks to resolve the tensions that have been evoked by the appearance of conflicting provinces of value meaning.

For those entering into a social world characterized by such a conflict of interpretations, there may be the tendency to seek to retypify the world in the light of alternative traditions which become experiential horizons for interpretation and action. In the present, for example, there are numerous experiential and interpretational horizons surrounding sexuality, marriage, and parenting, as well as work, leisure, and religious experience. In each of these cases there may be a significant generational difference in the way projects are interpreted and related to previously dominant value paradigms. Conflicts of interpretation highlight a dimension of decision and choice which proceeds, not routinely, but rather in a self-conscious fashion.

SELF-CONSCIOUS INTERPRETING

It is during periods of social change or personal crisis that the taken-for-granted sequences we have described are rendered problematic, and that which was routine becomes the object of conscious and often anxious attention. At these points in individual biography or social history, both selves and groups seek to reinterpret their situation and embody their action in new forms. Examples of such personal crises in our society would include divorce, the anticipation of death, retirement, loss of employment, incapacitating disease, and so on. Social changes which amount to the shifting in world horizons and value paradigms, and which also have an impact at the level of individual experience, would include the conquest and attempted cultural destruction of Native American tribes and its aftermath; wars that are not completely captured by a dominant horizon of meaning, such as the Korean and Vietnam wars; political and constitutional crises, such as Watergate, and so on.

In such situations the taken-for-granted projects, the routinized system of means and ends which seem appropriate to realize projects, the structure of typifications which formerly constituted the portion of the social world undergoing crisis, and the symbols which routinely evoked the experience of value undergo fundamental shifts. Confusion arises and the projects that once stood routinely to choice and oriented action disappear or change as themes organizing the moral life and moral experience. Such widespread crisis forces individuals and groups to "stop and take thought." At the level of individual experience, what this amounts to is the search for a new identity. A description of the elements of this search and the forms of interpretation which it involves will prepare the way for further illuminating the processes of decision and choice.[1]

The sense of identity which is threatened during times of crisis has two sides that constitute its reality. First, it is formed as the self builds up a consistent picture of its own past. This picture is sedimented in experience and forms the pregiven context for experience and action in the present. We do not normally have to engage in conscious acts of recollection or acts of projection in order to fill in our sense of past and our anticipation of future. Until a problematic situation intervenes, personal biography and an expectation of a continuity in our identity in future action proceeds to be constituted routinely in experience. Second, as action unfolds in the social world in the light of a project the self routinely appropriates action as its own. In an act of reflection, the self can retrospectively grasp its acts, claiming them as its own. "These were my acts," is an affirmation of identity. In most cases, however, conscious acts of reflection are not involved; the routine sedimentation that structures experience as it runs off gives rise to a sense of identification with our acts which is an unquestioned aspect of experience.

---

1. Some of the material that follows is based on my article, "Interpreting and Projecting: Two Elements of the Self as Moral Agent," *Journal of the American Academy of Religion* 41, 1 (1973): 18-29. I have obviously been influenced in this article by the analysis of Alfred Schutz, "Choosing among Projects of Action," CP, Vol. I, pp. 67-96; and by Paul Ricoeur's analysis in *Freedom and Nature: The Voluntary and the Involuntary*, trans. Erazim V. Kohák (Evanston, Ill.: Northwestern University Press, 1966), pp. 135 ff. Other influences include Stuart Hampshire's account of desire in *Freedom of the Individual* (New York: Harper & Row, 1965), pp. 34 ff.; Jean Nabert's work in *Elements for an Ethic*, trans. William J. Petrek (Evanston, Ill.: Northwestern University Press, 1969); and Raymond Polin's work on the relationship between imagination and the moral life in *La création des valeurs* (Paris: Presses Universitaires de France, 1952).

Self-conscious acts of interpretation arise as the self struggles to orient itself within an alien situation. The crisis which has enveloped the self and its social world has put a question mark over previous self-interpretations. The self has become a stranger to itself. The interpretative struggles that ensue involve imaginative variations by which the self seeks a new resolution of its identity. This process has three main phases which must be grasped. First, there is active reconstitution in memory of the self's past which has been put into question by crisis. As agony deepens within the self, it finds itself locked in a struggle between different interpretations of its own past. Out of this conflict emerges a second stage: the development of a new interpretation which becomes increasingly dominant in experience. The development of such an interpretation is not only dependent upon acts of judgment made by the self, but also involves interaction with others in the social world. The third stage involves a recession of possibilities which had once competed for dominance. The outcome of these three phases may be a new sense of integrity and identity. An exposition of these three phases will bring us closer to an understanding of the acting self as a self-conscious moral agent.

The center of the self's crisis lies in the partial or almost total disintegration of previously accepted self-images and a consequent inability to recognize itself in its own acts. This sense of alienation drives the self into its own memory, there actively to recollect the sedimented experiences that have led to its subjective impasse. Reproduction in memory brings the self into the presence of an inner terrain composed of the sometimes twisted paths forming the major outlines of remembered acts. Even at this level the self's survey is a complex interpretative process. The clear lines of action, the significant turning points, the decisions that brought about fateful consequences—all are recollections of the same self who once intended the course of action in the light of a project, turned down one path rather than another, made the crucial decision. From this viewpoint the layers of remembered experience, exposed by recollection, are the interpreted residue of what was once the projected action of the self.

As the process of retrospective interpreting continues, the self breaks down the larger themes of remembered experience into their component parts. At this juncture, imaginative variation may intervene and, to its consternation, the self finds that it is not a single past which is remembered, but rather many possible interpretations of the past. As the imagining self takes priority over the remembering self, familiar terrain which was once the subject of recollection may become alien ground. The play of imagination arranges previously interpreted images of the past into new configurations. Each of these possible interpretations has its own plausibility, and as the possibilities multiply, the self is driven deeper into its own agony. Which of the several interpretations is to become thematic for a new self-interpretation? Which of these themes will restore a sense of identity? Which interpretation is true to lived experience as it "really was"? These and other questions press the self from one side and then another as it seeks to resolve the conflicting interpretations oscillating in imagination.

Gradually the self becomes aware of the mystery and complexity of its action. In arranging and rearranging the levels of memory, new interpretations of formerly interpreted acts and motives become visible. New connections between acts that formerly looked disconnected appear. There are echoes of possible identity patterns which resonate in imagination, leading to the anxious thought that the self might not have been what it thought it was. In its anxiety the self wanders from one possible interpretation to another in what seems an endless labyrinth of imagining memories.

At this point it is important to make clear that neither remembering nor imagining is neutral. Both are activities of an anxious and interested self. In its pain the self may engage, for example, in imagining in the "optative mode."[2] This is to entertain wishful fantasies concerning the past: "Oh, how I wish it had been thus and so," or "How I wish it could have been thus and so." These two statements distinguish pure fantasy from imagination seeking a more realistic interpretation. Pure fantasy

2. Schutz, CP, Vol. I, pp. 72–73.

leads the self to imagine its past in ways which are dominated by the power of the wish images. A more realistic imagination emerges when the self, while assigning reality to particular meaning configurations concerning the past, still wishes they could have been otherwise. Pure fantasy and realistic imagining may also be distinguished from fancying in the defensive mode. In this case the self engages in defensive scenarios which often obscure rather than clarify the process of self-interpretation. Through this activity, the self seeks either to protect itself from painful awareness or to justify itself in relation to a preferred interpretation of its own past.

The emergence of the second stage in which the self is able to thematize its experience in terms of a new interpretation follows as a consequence of the activities we have described up to this point. Thus far the self has, by imaginal variation, sought to typify the past in new ways. Although we began the description by looking at the way the dynamics of interpretation appear in inner time, none of these dynamics is ever finally dissociated from the social world. The attempt to create new typifications and fill them with autobiographical significance may take many forms in its relation to the social world. An individual may, for example, seek psychotherapy in the struggle to retypify experience; or an individual may associate with certain groups or moral communities in an attempt to arrive at a resolute interpretation; or the self may become immersed in one or more traditions representing the sociocultural past in an attempt to arrive at a new interpretation.

The depth of the crisis may be so great that the process of retypifying the social world may be related to a recovery, renewal, or creation of symbols that evoke in experience value meanings which have disappeared as a consequence of the crisis. In this part of the struggle, the self may find that past traditions and their symbols of moral value may become, through imaginative entry into them, occasions for fresh experiences of value. Or, again, the individual may join a group that celebrates liturgically meanings associated with certain provinces of value. Granting the accent of reality to such provinces of meaning may become, for the self, an occasion for the appearance of a new theme which gives a sense of renewed integrity and identity.

The claim here is that when the self has evolved to the point where experience is formed not only in the light of new typifications, but also in the light of a new paradigm of value meaning, then interpretation will reach a significant level of stability. Until this level is achieved, the self will be pushed by its inclination and desire, by its thinking in the optative or defensive mode, or by its pure fantasy, which may approach the borders of madness. The weighting of possible interpretations of the self's past must finally be influenced by the achievement of a sensibility that arises out of the experiential power of a province of value meanings. That this horizon may also be related in complex ways to other provinces, such as the religious, is something we take for granted but which is not the explicit subject of the analysis at this juncture.

As the self increasingly centers on one dominant theme which interprets the past, the oscillation among possibilities gradually subsides. This signals the third stage, in which rejected possibilities of interpretation are retained in memory but begin to recede below the level of awareness as a consequence of the appearance of a stable interpretation. Even though the crisis may be solved temporarily, it is not without ambiguity. Between the oscillation of possibilities and their recession lies a zone through which the self must pass. Even though a new interpretation has become dominant, echoes of remembered but rejected possibilities remain. Affective attachments to one and then another resonate in the depths of the self. The new interpretation is too fresh to be deeply imprinted at the center of the self. Thus in the darkness, at the edges of consciousness, other possibilities threaten to prove to the self that, after all, they were valid.

The suffering of the self continues, even though its primary agony has been partly relieved. It is only as possibilities recede to a level of forgotten and affectively neutral realities that the self can appropriate a complete sense of identity. Identity is, however, always resolved temporarily, "until further notice." If crisis eclipses identity again, then the conscious process of retrospective interpreting may begin anew. Indeed, as should now be clear, this is a continual process which proceeds at both a routine and a self-conscious level at one and the same time.

We have highlighted the process by reference to a radical crisis of identity in order to bring into view the operation of elements which had, up to this point, been seen only at the level of routinization. As we have interpreted the self, it becomes clear that the achievement of a sense of integrity and identity is an essential phase in the preparation of the agent for action and choice.

SELF-CONSCIOUS PROJECTING

We have described the acting self as moral agent in terms of the struggle to interpret the past and achieve a sense of identity. Processes of decision and choice, and the grounds of their possibility in the self, have been exposed partially. What we must now do is describe decision and choice as these relate to projects, especially when projects are oriented to particular horizons of value meaning.

As fully self-conscious activity, projecting arises when taken-for-granted projects become problematic. This point raises an issue which must be clarified in order to avoid confusion. Even though the activities of interpretation and projection have been distinguished for purposes of description, they are phases in experience that interpenetrate. In facing a concrete crisis which both affects the sense of identity and disturbs routinized decision and choice by rendering projects problematic, the self is actually involved simultaneously in attempts to interpret its past and project new alternatives for action. And even though the crisis of identity and action may be deep, there are horizons of identity and action that remain routinized and are the presupposition for a minimal continuity in experience.

For example, even though the imposed themes of the death of an important other, divorce, or loss of career may put a question mark over much that was routinized in experience, the self is still usually able to function at such basic levels as acquiring adequate nutrition, maintaining communication with others, engaging in bodily movements, and so on. The crisis may be so deep, of course, that even these routinized interpretations and projections may be disturbed. In such cases, the agent is incapacitated in so many areas that a recovery of identity and envisioning of projects to guide decision and choice may be impossible. If such a condition persists in the experience of individuals, then we approach the border beyond which it is impossible to speak of a self; rather, we have to describe the disintegration of the self.

If we begin description at the level of individual experience, assuming a crisis which has rendered routinized projects problematic, then we can broaden the analysis to include relevant dimensions of the social world as we did in the treatment of interpretation. There are three phases that must be described: the competition of possibilities, the emergence of a dominant project, and the recession of possibilities.

In the first phase, the self portrays to itself images of differing possibilities for action. Because these possibilities are pictures of anticipated events, not recollections of past experience, their reality is constituted by the activity of the self in the imaginal-projective mode. Furthermore, such projections are characterized by the time structure described earlier: they are portrayals of acts as if they had already happened. As these possibilities multiply in experience, the imagining self engages in creative action, allowing fantasy to play over the possibilities, breaking them down into their component parts, and recombining them in new ways. In this process not only do new possibilities arise, but also new connections between familiar possibilities become visible. Projecting of this sort entangles the self in anxiety toward the future which is comparable to its agony over the past. Which of these possible futures should be brought into being in the social world? Which will most adequately embody the identity which has emerged as a consequence of retrospective interpreting? Which project or set of interrelated projects is most consistent with the horizon of value meanings evoked in the self's experience? These questions confront the self as it enters the struggle among competing possibilities.

As each possibility is articulated in imagination, there is a struggle in the self to order these projects in such a way that a choice will be forthcoming. Prior to any concrete choice which releases a project into the social world, there is the activity of deliberation which prepares the self for an integral decision in relation to competing possibilities. Three aspects of this deliberative process will be described here: first, an analysis of desire in relation to projected actions; second, an assessment of the project in light of a coherent province of value meaning; and, finally, a consideration of the way in which each possibility coheres with the emerging sense of identity. These three aspects of deliberation are distinguished with greater precision than they would be in the actual decision process of an incarnate self; and they do not all necessarily occur in the sequence described. The description is a typification of a process rich with variation and content which can only be illuminated, not fully captured, through analysis.

As each possibility is articulated by the imagining self, the ebb and flow of desire fills experience. Some possibilities appear more attractive than others and draw the self toward action through the lure of inclination. If deliberation continues, however, the self is able further to interrogate its desire. Of course, there are instances in experience where inclination captures a project and decision and choice are compressed in such a way that action flows without further reflection. If desire is interrogated, then tendencies are revealed which allow the self to identify projects that arise out of either pure desire or fantasies in the pure sense or in the defensive mode. As the imagining self is disciplined by reflection, it is prepared to enter into consideration of the tension that may be present between the lure of desire and the value meanings evoked in experience by symbols in a dominant paradigm of value.

If, for example, the paradigm by which the self interrogates its desire is teleological in form, then an assessment of the consequences of each imagined possibility becomes critical. Here the self pictures consequences of each possible future and compares the flow of imagined consequences with its apprehension of value. As the self considers consequences, combining and rearranging them in the imagination, some appear closer to the self's primary value paradigm than others. Then a new combination appears and the configuration which had appeared plausible is rendered problematic. It is important to note that the assessment of consequences in relation to imagined projects is of a special sort, since it occurs within the stream of consciousness itself. The self makes connections between imagined events and consequences which may have no actual connection or causal relationship when the project is released into the social world. The social world is so complex that the possible consequences imagined by the self may not be forthcoming—or they may appear in a form different from that which was anticipated in imagination.

If the self is more deeply conditioned by a deontological value paradigm, then consideration of consequences may not be at the center of attention. Rather, choice among projects will proceed more along the lines of considering the way each conforms or fails to conform to the notion of duty or obedience to law. And if the paradigm is relatively coherent in terms of its classical formulation, then there may be a tension between duty and desire in the self's decision process.

Here again reflections of a self which interprets itself deontologically are constructions within internal time and do not necessarily represent the form action will take when it is shaped in the social world in the light of a project. Even though deontological horizons of value may take their rise in the primordial experience of the other, it is still the case that experience and action can never be abstracted completely from their teleological elements, as we have shown. Thus an image of the self obeying a law or conforming to duty is itself a project which fantasizes action in the future perfect tense and which functions in the deliberative process to prepare the self for action and choice. That the project is interpreted in relation to a deontological province of value makes it no less a project.

Finally, if moral experience is conditioned by the symbol of responsibility, then the root question will be the imagination of action which relates in an appropriate manner to the responses of others within an ongoing social context. Attention to action in the light of this value paradigm will stimulate the imagining self in its deliberation to portray varying interpretations of what is going on in order to make a judgment about what might be the most fitting response. This horizon of value will motivate the self in its deliberation to assess projects in the light of their capacity to realize and fulfill relationships and others rather than to thwart and destroy them.[3]

As the desiring–imagining self struggles with competing possibilities in the light of these various horizons of value meaning, it also engages in the third activity mentioned earlier, which is to assess the projects in relation to the emerging sense of identity achieved by retrospective interpreting. Since the self is seeking to resolve not only a choice among projects but also an identity crisis, action must be imaged in such a way that it coheres with newly emerging self-understandings. Thus the self imagines not only its future acts in the light of a particular value paradigm, but also possible versions of itself. It is not enough that the self resolve competing possibilities into a single project or projects. The projects must also at least appear to embody the self-understanding achieved by retrospective interpreting. That such embodiment is never entirely possible does not relieve the pressure in the self. At least the belief that identity will be coherent in the imagined project is a minimal condition for moving closer to the release of the project into the social world.

The movement of the deliberative process through these three dimensions may push the self toward the second major stage on the way toward action and choice: the emergence of a dominant project. As the weighting of possibilities continues, the self grows and matures in its deliberation until one project or structure of projects begins to displace the others. This project or projects will finally emerge as that which reflects most coherently the value paradigm that forms the horizon of the self's interpretation and embodies most clearly the sense of identity that is being achieved by the self. The emergence of a dominant project is, of course, related in the same way as was interpretation to significant others and groups in the social world. Most fundamentally, this emergence is dependent upon the interaction between the value sensibility of the individual and a paradigm of value which is sedimented in the social world and coexperienced by others.

---

3. The analysis could be extended, of course, to paradigms which emphasize utilitarian motifs or notions of virtue.

If the self is successful in resolving competing possibilities into a single project or structure of projects, then the final stage in the movement toward action comes into view. Rejected possibilities begin to recede, gradually sinking back toward the outer horizons of awareness, and finally becoming sedimented in experience beyond our immediate grasp. There they remain as possibilities once considered by the self, and they are capable of being reconstituted in memory and may again become the subject of reflective awareness. For example, if an inconsistency appears between project and unfolding action, the self may begin a review of its judgments and acts. The longer this process continues, the greater the chance that the self will sink again into a morass of competing possibilities. Then the memory of rejected projects may rise to challenge the self's judgments, further threatening the stability it has achieved. The outcome of these tendencies may be a new series of projections and, in the case of a severe crisis, a renewal of retrospective interpreting.

Up to this point the process of deliberation has been represented as unfolding in inner time as the self gradually moves toward a decision in favor of one project, excluding others from view. Action which is guided by the emerging project flows now into the social world. When the self gears into the world, then the situation changes. No longer are identity and commitment representations in imagination. Identity and value meanings now interact within the intricate network of the social world, conforming to or coming into conflict with other agents and their projects. But as the activity of interpreting and projecting was formative for the self, so the action of the self as it impresses itself upon the world is innovative. The action of the self adds something new to the world and the world is changed by this action.

We have now achieved at least a partial vision of the acting self as moral agent. The argument portrayed the acting self as interpreting itself and orienting its actions by means of projects which find their ground in horizons of value meaning evoked in experience by symbols. The self in its acting is oriented by many different projects and is continually engaged in interpretative acts. The sum total of this process is the life-plan and self-understanding of an individual at any given point in time. For some, action may be oriented by interpreting and projecting which is grounded in a coherent province of value meaning; for others, interpreting and projecting may be grounded in a horizon of value which is fundamentally conditioned by a sense of reality mediated by the symbols of a religious tradition; for still others, moral experience and action may be oriented by projects that are grounded in more fragmented value sensibilities. In all of these instances, individual agents who act do so in the social world and find themselves in conflict with or in relative conformity to particular value paradigms which are sedimented in the experience of others and which appear as intersubjective realities dialectically related to individual moral experience.

We also emphasized the innovative power of the self as moral agent. A description of freedom emerged as we considered the capacity of the self to reinterpret its past and to project alternative visions of its future. The same capacity is present in the social world. Thus at both levels there are open horizons of possibility lying beyond any given routinization of moral experience or any particular moral tradition. These open horizons are expressions of the precarious nature of the human world, as well as the capacity of the self to constitute and reconstitute a world. In such activity the nature of the human being is revealed in some of its complexity and final mystery. In the process of constituting a world, there emerge the many worlds of experience corresponding to multiple levels of awareness which are indigenous to consciousness. One of these levels apprehends the world in terms of various horizons of value.

In the light of this analysis we cannot properly say, in an exclusive manner, that human beings either discover values or originate them. Both statements must be taken together as an expression of the dialectic between the capacity for symbolic awareness and the objects of that awareness which characterize moral experience. The analysis of the origination of value is at the same time a discussion of the grounds in the human being which make such appearances of value possible. This amounts to saying that the human being is a valuing being and that the social world is value-laden. This is an expression of fundamental human nature and the essential structure of the human social world.

The final chapter will pick up the themes of deliberation and choice as they appear within the context of moral communities. As it has been developed in previous chapters, the argument has alluded to, but has not made explicit, what constitutes the nature of moral communities. When this problem has been clarified, we will be able to understand the part moral discourse plays in these communities not only in relation to decision and choice, but also in relation to inducing social change or maintaining a particular social order. The theme of interpretation, introduced as an element essential to moral agency, will appear again as an activity central to moral discernment.

VI

Moral Discourse in the Social World

THE SOCIAL WORLD has been interpreted as a reality composed of unities of meaning that are coexperienced intersubjectively and are mediated by shared types and symbols. What we call institutions, such as the family and the state, as well as social projects, such as making war and collecting taxes, are examples of such important unities of meaning. These realities are maintained in experience through being widely shared, and they are changed by changing the meanings evoked in the experience of individuals who compose a group. Changes in the social world are changes in the unities of typical and symbolic meaning which constitute that world.

This perspective sheds light upon a type of change that is of central importance for this study. Here we have in view changes in the social world that are motivated by interpretation and projection which embody particular provinces of value meaning. A description of how such changes occur will be illustrated by historical and contemporary examples, but first it is necessary to provide a preliminary definition of moral communities and moral discourse consistent with the point of view developed in the previous chapters.

MORAL COMMUNITIES

At a formal level, moral communities are constituted by shared value meanings which are relatively consistent and which are evoked in the experience of individuals belonging to determinate groups. Provinces of value meaning may be deeply routinized in experience, as we have seen, or they may become objects of self-conscious attention. In either case, the identity and distinctiveness, as well as the temporal duration of moral communities are made possible by shared paradigms of value meaning. At a material level, moral communities achieve their determinate shape according to the content of the value meanings which are symbolically apprehended.

It is important to note that this view of moral communities does not presuppose the necessity of face-to-face relations, although it does not exclude this important aspect either. Especially in modern societies, with their complex interrelations and systems of mass communication, it is possible for moral communities to be constituted of contemporaries who are widely separated in physical and social space. The same social world can typically be grasped by contemporaries, and provinces of value meaning can be evoked in their experience by means of symbolic pairing. Types and symbols do not require proximity for their shared meaning to coordinate experience, action, and interpretation. A moral community may ritually rehearse a particular province of value meaning in a face-to-face or small group context, to be sure. But a moral community may also arise as a consequence of the ritual rehearsal of value meanings that are carried by various systems of mass communication. That this is possible is clearly and decisively illustrated every time a political or religious leader is able, through appealing to widely shared symbols, to evoke concrete experiences of value in individuals widely separated in both social and physical space. When this occurs, the community thus constituted may properly be called a moral community.

MORAL DISCOURSE

Moral discourse has generally been understood to refer to the activity by which moral agents arrive at normative judgments. A recent definition proposes that moral discourse appears when persons gather "with the explicit intention to survey and critically discuss their personal and social responsibilities in the light of moral convictions about which there is some consensus and to which there is some loyalty."[1] The analysis in this section will trace this general understanding of moral discourse to its roots in structures that have previously received description. Again the view of types and symbols will be the beginning point for developing an analysis of moral discourse in the social world.

As was previously argued, the social world arises from and is apprehended by acts of typifying consciousness. At this level, the unities of meaning that form the social world appear in experience as determinate, taken-for-granted realities. When widely shared, this world is the substance of the culture, the institutions, and the worldview which characterizes the experience of a people. At a higher level, this social world is fringed with meanings that are symbolically evoked in the experience of individuals. These meanings arise as a consequence of multivalent symbols, spanning more than one province of meaning, and bring additional dimensions of transcendence to bear upon the everyday world. Symbols may evoke meanings that relate to religious, aesthetic, and evaluative regions, among others. It is through further analysis of the relation between the typical and symbolic levels of the social world that a preliminary understanding of moral discourse arises.

Typifying consciousness deals with the level of referential meaning in the sense that the unities of meaning thus constituted are taken to describe the social world as it actually is. As long as the elements of the social world are experienced in a coherent manner, action and communication unfold routinely. The realities mediated by symbols may also be routinized at a level of considerable depth in particular societies. When this is the case, there is some relative coherence between the world as typified and the meanings that are symbolically paired with provinces of religion and value meaning, for example. To use other language, the understanding of the relationship between fact and value is

---

1. James M. Gustafson, *The Church as Moral Decision-Maker* (Philadelphia: Pilgrim Press, 1970), p. 84. The definition which Gustafson proposes applies formally to moral discourse, as it appears not only within religious groups but also within other sorts of human associations.

relatively lacking in tension. In such a social world, horizons of symbolic meaning inform and infuse horizons of typical meaning, providing dimensions of depth to individual experience. That these dimensions are routinized does not diminish their significance for enriching individual experience.

As a self-conscious activity, moral discourse arises when a disjunction appears between the world as typified and levels of meaning relating to provinces of value. Two phases of this process will be illustrated in the examples that follow: first, there is the struggle among individuals and groups to retypify the social world; and, second, there is a struggle to bring symbolic meanings critically to bear upon the world as it is typically apprehended. Thus understood, moral discourse is most clearly visible when taken-for-granted experience becomes problematic. As a process, however, it continues when experience is unproblematic.

For example, moral discourse occurs among relatively stable social groups and may function to reinforce shared understandings of fact and value. The process of moral discourse may also arise as a modality of justifying or defending a group position. This points toward the essential ambiguity of the moral life and shared paradigms of value. Values may be intended and achieve extensive reality status in the experience of large numbers of individuals, and yet these values and their social paradigms may embody concrete meanings which motivate the racial domination or economic exploitation of one group by another. Moral discourse may be related, that is, to paradigms of value meaning which might embody negative value when interpreted from the perspective of another value persuasion. The purpose of this chapter is to illuminate the dimensions of moral discourse within moral communities rather than to make normative judgments concerning the adequacy or appropriateness of any particular province of value meanings. The intention is analytical and is aimed at deeper understanding of moral communities and their discourse.

Since typical and symbolic meanings actually interpenetrate in the constitution of the social world, it is possible to separate them only for purposes of analytical clarity. But we may distinguish two moments or phases within moral discourse, one having to do with retypifying the social world and the other having to do with recovering the power and concreteness of the experience evoked by paradigms of value meaning. Within these two broad phases there is a further process which may also be highlighted through example and historical illustration. This we will define as the process of moral discernment, which in this analysis will refer to the act of taking the point of view of the other in an activity of interpretation.

THE CONFLICT OF INTERPRETATIONS

If we begin with the emergence of a problematic situation in the social world, then the first phase of moral discourse may be illustrated concretely. A problematic situation appears when fissures occur in the social consensus concerning the meaning structure of important sectors of the social world. Moral communities may initially engage in discourse and debate concerning what is believed to be the case about the social world. This phase is captured in the activity of reenvisioning or attempting to retypify sectors of the social world which have become problematic.

For example, moral communities are engaged in discourse at the present time on the issue of abortion. One of the central points in this discourse involves a conflict of interpretations over how to typify the process of the generation of human life. To further illustrate the arguments, it is possible to identify those who typify the product of conception as a human life from the point at which genetic uniqueness emerges, the union of egg and sperm.[2] It is significant to note that, for some who take this view, the moral arguments and judgments about the nature of the act of abortion are based upon a set of typifications concerning the beginning of human life which are derived from a

---

2. See, for instance, James M. Gustafson, "A Protestant Ethical Approach," in *The Morality of Abortion*, ed. John T. Noonan (Cambridge: Harvard University Press, 1970), pp. 101-22. This position, generally speaking, has also represented Roman Catholic thought on this subject.

scientific province of meaning. Other groups within the debate employ a scientific paradigm to make just the opposite point, namely, that genetic potentiality has to be realized at a certain (debatable) level in order for the qualities of human life to be present. For these groups, generally speaking, embryonic life must have developed fully into fetal life before the typification of "human life" is viewed as appropriate. It is clear that the process of typifying the beginning point of human life is an essential element in the interpretation of the nature of the act of abortion. If we are able at some point to typify fetal life as "human life," then the act of abortion may be related to the further typification "killing." At this point debates may arise concerning when one can kill legitimately, which gives rise to additional conflicts among typified structures of meaning in the social world, some of which are embodied in law.

Reenvisioning the nature of what is in the social world also moves at the level of reinterpreting typified social roles and taken-for-granted meaning structures concerning social position. At the present time in American society there is unfolding a complicated debate among individuals and moral communities concerning how to typify the social roles that structure relations between men and women. Received typifications, which embody modalities of subordination of women to men and sex-assigned role performances, are becoming increasingly problematic. Moral discourse has been most heated at this level, and also at the level at which typifications are embedded in language. Debates about "sexist language" are often debates about how to typify these broader roles and social relations. It is extremely important to understand that these debates have a direct impact upon a larger meaning structure which is a major social institution. These are, of course, the interrelated typifications which form an understanding of the family in American society. Here the process of reenvisioning penetrates deeply into the self-understanding and identity patterns of large numbers of individuals. Because the typifications which are problematic are so extensive and structure such a large sector of the social world, discourse on this issue is understandably intense.

Another interesting contemporary conflict of interpretations concerns taken-for-granted assumptions about the nature of sexuality. Deep within our society there are widely shared understandings concerning the appropriateness of heterosexual relations and the inappropriateness or even perversity of homosexuality. Minority typifications have also been present, but only recently in our society have these interpretations come fully into view. For some groups, it is interesting that even for individuals who are homosexual the typifications by which identity is interpreted are often drawn from a scientific paradigm—psychoanalysis. In the light of this paradigm, both the interpreters of homosexuality and those who are homosexuals may view the reality of homosexuality as an aberration. Typified as a psychosocial disease, it is argued that the application of the knowledge and paradigms of psychology will function to cure the homosexual. By contrast, an interesting point of view has recently developed which interprets the scientific paradigm as inadequate for understanding the true nature of homosexuality. For those groups who reject psychoanalysis, moral discourse involves debate about what are believed to be more adequate typifications concerning the identity and meaning of homosexuality in our society.

An historical example which illustrates how social position can be variously typified is provided by the case of the Native Americans. During much of the nineteenth century, Native Americans were typically seen as a group in need of "civilizing and Christianizing." The intention of government policy came to rest in the attempt, through programs of enforced socialization, to transform tribal cultures, conforming them to images of what was believed to be a superior American culture. Language, religion, forms of marriage, and relationships to the land—all of which were meaning structures that composed what was left of tribal worldviews and self-understandings—were subjected to a process of forced retypification. Although the self-understanding and destiny of many Americans were expressed in these policies, there were dissenting voices, but these were unable to change the direction of public policy. It was not until the administration of Franklin D. Roosevelt, and more recently during debates about minorities in American society, that

121

Native Americans have been typified by whites according to their cultural uniqueness. Although this process is far from complete, the search is for typifications which more adequately reflect the cultural heritage and distinctiveness of Native Americans.[3] In these examples we have seen how important types and typification are in constituting the social world in a determinate manner. At one level the world is a complex structure of shared meanings which is brought into experience through typification; if the types by which the world is constituted become problematic, then a social crisis emerges which motivates what has been called reenvisioning or reinterpreting. Clearly, types play a central role in both the activity of interpretation, which may proceed routinely, and the activity of reinterpretation, which arises in response to an emergence of the problematic. An important phase of moral discourse within moral communities involves the interpretation and reinterpretation of the nature of the social world. Conflicts of interpretation are precisely conflicts about the meaning of the social world as it is constituted by typifying consciousness.

Another historical illustration will serve to highlight additional features of this first phase of moral discourse. These features have to do with typifications by which we grasp others in the social world and also through which we enter into the world of predecessors. We may take the example of the Vietnam War, which illustrates a type of social change that was stimulated by moral discourse at both the typical and the symbolic levels.[4]

The constitution of a public interpretation of reality which binds action and interpretation, rendering it routine, is necessary to coordinate the action of a collectivity, such as a nation-state. This is especially the case if the action of the collec-

3. These generalizations are based on interpretations of government documents and communications of the period. I have dealt with this issue in *Mission among the Blackfeet* (Norman: Oklahoma University Press, 1971), ch. VI.
4. I employed this illustration in a slightly different form in "The Human Center: Moral Discourse in the Social World," *Journal of Religious Ethics* 5, 2 (1977): 201-2.

tivity involves prosecuting a war. The intentions and interpretations of typified others, such as the president, or typified groups, such as the Congress or the joint chiefs of staff, are extremely important elements in constituting a war as a widely shared social project. The intentions and motives of contemporaries, such as political and military leaders, are apprehended typically by citizens. If the typical understanding of the meaning of the war is widely shared, then the national project achieves sufficient legitimacy to be able to unfold without extremely divisive social conflict.

In the case of Vietnam, there was a period when the constructs by which individuals understood the purposes of the nation in relation to typified collectivities (the Viet Cong) or individuals (Ho Chi Minh) remained powerful enough to constitute a socially legitimated public interpretation of reality. Such constructs enabled government (which, for the citizen, means typified others such as the president, or groups, such as the Congress) to communicate with individuals (which, for the government, means typified others called citizens) about the national purposes in relation to the war.

As long as a public interpretation of the war was widely shared, citizens were expected to respond routinely to tax levies to support the war and provide personnel to fight. Change began when small groups, and then increasingly larger groups, began to retypify the social world. Such activity actually changed the character of the social world precisely because of the way it is constituted in experience. The arena of change was small in the beginning but spread until an entire portion of the taken-for-granted social world collapsed. At first, individuals banded together to oppose the public interpretation of the war. Students and faculty on campuses, as well as voluntary associations such as churches, began a process of moral discourse. The history of Vietnam and the reasons for national involvement were interpreted and reinterpreted until finally there was no clear vision concerning the reasons for entering the war or the reasons for remaining. The result of moral discourse at the level of retypification was a collapse of meaning structures that enabled the nation to fight the war.

An important element that caused the collapse of these meaning structures was the stimulation of a process of retypifying the motives of contemporaries and the meaning of the national purpose. In the former case, Ho Chi Minh may be reinterpreted as a folk hero rather than an embodiment of Communism; and the Viet Cong may be reinterpreted as prosecutors of a civil war rather than as aggressors against freedom. At a broader level, the American national image was interpreted in the light of past colonial action. Conceiving of the nation as the defender of freedom around the world became an increasingly difficult meaning structure to maintain. Also, the actions and motives of important contemporaries, such as the president, lost legitimacy and increasingly became the subject of reinterpretation.

The introduction of questions about the past presses toward typifications of another order. At this level we have to do not with the actions of contemporaries but rather with the actions of predecessors and their meaning for responding to the present. For instance, as moral discourse about Vietnam matured, retypifying gradually began to involve the interpretation of significant political predecessors and events. Partly through the stimulus of the writings of intellectuals, persons were led to an examination of their past. Was not the beginning of America marked by a revolution? If this was the case, then what has happened to this part of the national heritage? For some, it appeared that Americans had forgotten their revolutionary tradition and had created an ossified, conservative state which could not recognize or respond to movements for freedom within or without the national borders. As interpretation of the past continued, there was an accompanying struggle to identify the primary values believed to have been embodied by the predecessors. Here moral discourse attempted to typify past traditions of value. The outcome of this particular process was a national withdrawal from the war and the emergence of attempts to grasp the meaning of national involvement and to project a vision of national destiny. This process has not yet come to rest in a widely shared interpreted meaning structure.

Attempts to retypify the social world have also risen in connection with the emergence of ecological crises. These debates involve not only attempts to typify nature in a different manner, so that human relationships to the natural environment can be understood more symbiotically rather than in terms of a competitive–dominant model of meaning, but also an envisioning of the world for the sake of future generations. In this case, the lure of successors and the desire that the ecological possibilities for their existence be maintained are important themes in the discourse of groups that are locked in a conflict of interpretation on these issues.

By appealing to diverse examples, we have illustrated some of the important elements in the phase of moral discourse that involves reenvisioning the social world. At this level the debates largely concern referential meanings which, taken together, formed a particular definition of the situation. We turn now to the second dimension of moral discourse, which has to do with the constitution of a fresh sensibility concerning value meanings and moral traditions. Often this process involves conflicts at the symbolic level of the social world.

SYMBOLIC CONFLICTS

Once again it needs to be emphasized that types and symbols interact to constitute in experience the dimensions of meaning that compose the social world. The precise character of that interaction has not been the focus of attention, but now it is necessary to make clear that the first phase of moral discourse always interacts with and in fact may be precipitated by the apprehension of a moral tradition or by the irruption of a horizon of value meanings which calls into question previously taken-for-granted typifications. In either case, the appearance of the experience of value provides the grounds and the motivation for the exercise of moral judgment. Normative critiques of the social world, which have previously been taken for granted but which have now become problematic, must be traced to their roots in shared paradigms of value meaning.

To return to the case of abortion, the conflict of interpretation may now be seen as it is embedded in a conflict of value at the symbolic level. This deeper conflict is of the nature of tension between two or more shared paradigms of value meaning. If moral discourse moves along the lines of typifying the beginning of human life at the point of conception, and if the paradigm of value meaning which is shared in a moral community is deontological in content, for example, then there is likely to emerge a defense of fetal rights which puts the burden of proof on any who would seek to take that life through an act of abortion. Even though the fetus may not be typified as a "person," there will still be the designation "human life," which tends to qualify the act of abortion as an act of killing. A further element in a shared province of deontological value meanings may be a deep bias toward protection of life and prohibitions against the direct killing of another human being. Such value meanings authorize and motivate projects at the concrete level of moral action; the operation of this general value paradigm appears incarnate in the life of the moral agent.

The depth of these value conflicts may be illustrated by analyzing briefly, and in an ideal-typical manner, some of the differences that may appear if the issue of abortion is the subject of moral discourse rooted in a utilitarian paradigm. Generally speaking, this horizon of value meanings would give greater consideration to situational contexts and to considerations of the consequences of action than would the deontological paradigm. Fetal life may have some value, although that value is not usually rooted in an argument that locates the beginning of human life at conception. In any case, courses of action and projects will be authorized by showing the impact they have upon persons and situations rather than imagining life in terms of obedience to rules or conformity to moral law. For instance, the psychological health of the mother, the economic and social condition of the family, and even the general considerations of the world population may become contexts within which values emerge that must be balanced against the life of the fetus. Consequential reasoning proceeding from one or more of these base points may end in justifying the act of abortion for the sake of greater ends or goods to be realized.

In the case of either deontology or utilitarianism, the power of the symbols that evoke these respective experiences of value will be brought to bear upon the typifications surrounding and defining the act of abortion. As moral discourse proceeds, there will be pressure within moral communities to bring typical meanings into conformity with the symbolic meanings mediated in their respective moral traditions. What is typically believed to be the case at the referential level receives its final authorization in terms of levels of symbolic meaning. In other language, that which is, is grounded in and legitimated by a horizon of value meanings.

In instances where large portions of the social world have become problematic, horizons of value may themselves become problematic. Conflicts of value may drive moral communities toward a deeper hermeneutic of their own value traditions in an attempt to recover a sense of symbolic power. It is at this point that the lone prophet or charismatic leader may arise to propose the interpretative horizon which will capture the moral imagination of the members of a collectivity. At this juncture, moral discourse involves the reinterpretation of a previously held moral tradition or, in extreme cases, the origination of new moral traditions.

In the light of this analysis, moral discourse in the social world involves shaping typified meanings in reference to a transcendent center of value meanings which is powerfully evoked in the experience of members of a moral community. In addition to reenvisioning the social world, moral discourse leads to the recommendation of social projects that are understood to be in correspondence with meanings apprehended through intending the world in the light of a horizon of value.

The tendency of the process of moral discourse is to move experience from the problematic to the nonproblematic, from crisis to routinization. If the process of moral discourse is successful in resolving that which is problematic, then the outcome will be typical and symbolic closure. The social world will tend to sink again into the realm of taken-for-granted sequences; and the value meanings evoked in experience will become so routinized that interpretation and projection will unfold in the social world without taking thought. The world as it is experienced typically is perceived to be in harmony with the world as it is apprehended symbolically.

MORAL DISCERNMENT

Conflicts of interpretation and symbolic conflicts have been analyzed as aspects of self-conscious moral discourse. Through moral discourse, individuals seek to achieve an adequate interpretation of what is going on (typical, referential meaning) and to bring that interpretation into conformity with what is apprehended at the symbolic level. Central to this process is an element which must be brought more clearly into view. This is the activity of moral discernment, which is viewed here as an act of imagination through which we take the point of view of the other. Taking the point of view of the other has an important impact upon our reading of what is going on (interpretation), and it can also affect the level of experience which is symbolically mediated.

Before outlining the dimensions of moral discernment that are pertinent to this treatment, it is necessary briefly to recall that the capacity to take the point of view of the other is given as a part of the structure of agency. Because we are fundamentally social beings, it is possible to enter into the other's stream of consciousness through various acts of communication. On the basis of this general capacity, moral discernment involves the additional qualification of imaginative entry into another's experience in order to discover what might be the most appropriate action or relationship with that other. Moral discernment may function at any point along the continuum from face-to-face relations to more anonymous relations among contemporaries. In the case of face-to-face relations, it is obviously easier to test the adequacy of moral imagination by continual interaction with the other.

Moral discernment also participates fully in the essential ambiguity of the moral life. Taking the point of view of the other may be done within the context of a paradigm of value meanings and acts of interpretation which actually aim toward the distortion or suppression of the other; or moral discernment may aim toward the furtherance of the other's being and good. The force of this argument has been to show that both actions that are generally approved and those that may be generally disapproved proceed from interpreting and projecting in the light of horizons of value meanings. Interpretative and symbolic conflicts become intense precisely because they concern deeply held attitudes and experiences which are sustained by shared types and symbols in the social world. There is no way to mute this conflict or to deny that it has often led to acrimonious debate and even to violence. Another type of study would be required to deal with this complex and important issue. At this juncture we want simply to illustrate the importance of moral discernment in the process of moral discourse, leaving aside the difficult problem of the evaluation of alternative value horizons.

The view of moral discernment as an act through which we take the point of view of the other may be illustrated briefly by appeal to examples drawn from relations running from intimacy to greater degrees of anonymity. Beginning at the more anonymous side of the continuum, the first case illustrates how moral discernment may function in relation to others who are typified for purposes of constructing public policy. Again, Native Americans in our society are a group that illustrates this point. During the nineteenth and early twentieth centuries, when the policy of forced acculturation was being implemented, moral arguments for this policy often took the form of an appeal to the "best interests" of Native American people. Public officials who had responsibilities for Indian affairs seemed to typify Native Americans as a group that could enter American society only if they acquired the culture, the language, the religion, and the virtues of Americans. Some of the these arguments were quite sympathetic to the plight of tribal peoples in the throes of radical social change and viewed assimilation as the only viable social goal toward which policy should aim. This policy was justified, in part, by interpreting Native American life on the basis of imaginative entry into their experience. In this case, however, taking the point of view of the other actually turned out to be a straightforward affirmation of the superiority of American cultural values, which illustrates in an interesting way the ambiguity of moral discernment.[5]

Just the opposite point of view emerged, as has been noted, during the administration of Franklin D. Roosevelt. At the center of this policy shift was a process of moral discernment which envisioned the point of view of the other in a manner quite different from that envisioned during the earlier period of forced acculturation. Rather than the affirmation of the superiority of American cultural forms, a new appreciation and understanding of the meaning structures of the native world emerged. Native languages, religion, ceremonial life, and cultural values, once the object of suppression, were now affirmed and supported by the new policy. The shared social project had formerly been expressed in a policy of assimilation, but now the policy became that of toleration and cultural pluralism.[6]

This illustration makes clear the ambiguity of moral discernment and the diverse consequences it may have in the social world. The ambiguity of moral discernment is deepened in this case because public policy, when implemented, involves the use of social power. The policy of forced acculturation was ironic in the sense that it proposed a policy of culture destruction on the grounds of a vision of what were believed to be the best interests of the typified others who were the subjects of that policy. The point to be emphasized, however, is that both the policy of forced acculturation and the policy of culture affirmation and renewal were based upon broad processes of moral discourse as

5. It is interesting to note that moral discernment on the part of some has moved toward an interpretation of Native American culture which is supportive of the values of conservation and protection of the environment.

6. See, for example, John Collier, *Indians of the Americas* (New York: Mentor Books, 1947), ch. 14.

well as upon acts of moral discernment through which the point of view and the needs of the other were differently apprehended and evaluated.

Another case that illustrates the process of moral discernment at the level of public policy appeared during the mid-1960s, as a part of a debate about the needs of what was then known as the "Negro Family."[7] The debate essentially turned on conflicting perceptions of what the needs of these typified others really were. One type of moral discernment held that the black family, especially the family in poverty, ought to become an object of a sort of public therapy which would break the cycle of what was known as the "culture of poverty." By contrast, another type of moral discernment held that the basic need of poor black families was money, not therapy.

We previously described the process of moral discourse in relation to the Vietnam War, emphasizing particularly the conflict which was central to the struggle toward a more adequate typical and symbolic grasp of this situation. What needs further emphasis here is the way in which moral discernment shifted from a vision of the other as enemy to a vision of the other as victim. This change involved enormously complex factors, one of the most important of which was the mass communications media. The continual representation of organized violence against the Vietnamese people, night after night on the network news broadcasts, gradually affected the perceptions of what was going on. The fundamental structure of types, analyzed earlier, began to be threatened. Central to this process were acts of moral imagination by which the point of view of typical others was assimilated into what finally became an alternative view of national identity and destiny.

As a final example of moral discernment which moves toward the pole of more intimate relations, we may appeal to the

---

7. See Daniel P. Moynihan, *The Negro Family: The Case for National Action* (Washington, D.C., 1966). This document, originally prepared as a resource document for the 1966 White House Conference on Civil Rights, evoked lively and heated discussion of the issues.

medical context of care for dying patients. Typical expectations and interpretations attributed to dying persons, which tended to make the goal either the management of a disease complex or the defense of a body against its ultimate enemy, are being challenged by those who argue that taking the point of view of the dying person ought to inform specific actions within the caring context. Such acts of moral imagination also have their impact at the symbolic level. An alternative symbolism of the dying process is now coming into conflict with views that hold death as the great negative value to be conquered by technological medicine. This new symbolism is more holistic and accepting of the "natural" character of dying, and it seeks to enable dying persons to work through this process according to their own purposes and feelings.[8]

Taking the point of view of the other has been treated at the level of contemporaries who, individually or in groups, are the objects of typifying consciousness. The illustration of the dying person may be extended in order to bring into clear focus how moral discernment functions in the face-to-face relationship. The first and most obvious difference between taking the point of view of a concrete other and that of typified others is the possibility that moral imagination will be informed by a continuing process of primary communication. Typical others whose needs and conditions we imagine may not in actual fact be as we had imagined. In this case, the process of interpretation and projection may be based upon moral discernment which is more imaginal than realistic and which runs the risk of misinterpretation and inappropriate action.

Second, the consequence of primary communication can be the acquisition of detailed knowledge of the meaning structure which informs the other's experience. Such a deep sense of the concrete identity of the other can inform the process of interpretation and action in such a way that it may be more responsive to the actual meaning structures and experiences of the other. In

---

8. See David Barton, ed., *Dying and Death* (Baltimore: The Williams and Wilkins Co., 1977), esp. pt. 1. Barton, who is a physician and a psychiatrist, has developed a very sensitive analysis of this problem.

the case of a specific dying person, action may be informed by such intimate knowledge that the process of action will unfold, not in relation to abstract rules, but rather in relation to an ongoing process of discernment. Such abstractions as "Always tell the truth to dying patients" or "Pain is a negative experience to be avoided at all costs" will be qualified, sometimes quite radically, by the process of moral discernment within the face-to-face context.

Moral discernment is understood to be central to the process of moral discourse in the social world. It is that activity which challenges or defends how the social world is typically apprehended and, more particularly, how our relations with others are viewed. It is also that reality which can disturb experience in such a manner that root paradigms of value meaning and their experiential correlates are challenged. Such challenges often occur when the other performs a symbolic function, pairing our experience with a new horizon of value meaning.

The process of moral discourse and discernment is also extremely significant within the context of a modern society within which action and interpretation may be extended through bureaucratic social structures and mass communications. We remarked earlier that it was possible to act indirectly through such structures upon a social world which is widely separated from us in space. The constitution of moral communities within which discernment and discourse take place occurs by virtue of types and symbols that constitute unities of meaning which can be shared, even by those who are widely separated. Entry into such horizons of meaning is made possible by a ritual process which binds the moral experience of persons to particular paradigms of value.

THE RITUAL PROCESS

The sedimentation of typical and symbolic horizons of meaning by means of language, text, artifact, and art form make possible the continuity of a moral community over time. As long as moral experience remains unproblematic, the world as apprehended and evaluated is mediated generationally and maintained ritually. It is the ritual process which sustains moral communities, enabling them to move from the problematic to the routine in what is perhaps an endless rhythm, since experience is never completely closed and captured by the taken-for-granted.

The ritual process is that complex of action, embodied gesture, and language by means of which provinces of value meaning are maintained and periodically revivified.[9] Ritual does not, of course, flourish only in large corporate settings; there are ritual acts that appropriately apply to families and even to individuals. It is, however, through the ritual process that an individual, a family, a small group, or a larger corporate entity strengthens and renews the accent of reality granted to value sensibilities which are evoked in experience through the complex symbolic network of a particular province of value meaning. As long as moral sensibilities remain vital at the experiential level, the light from the paradigm of value will suffuse itself throughout other meaning networks and will qualify the way in which relationships to persons, groups, and nature are conceived.

The possibility for a migration of individual experience into the region of meanings characterized by a particular province of value is provided by the ritual process being concretely embodied in a moral community. The moral community is the locus for the rehearsal of concrete values which illuminate and condition the specific value judgments of individuals. The moral community is also the social correlate that is dialectically related to individual moral intentionality. Its reality is grounded in the typifying and symbolic capacities of human consciousness. But when types and symbols are coexperienced in a moral community, their reality sense is deepened and broad-

9. This is obviously a Durkheimian view of the function of ritual. Despite his positivism, I still find myself in agreement with Durkheim's views concerning the symbolic reality of society, although I reject his view that the referent of religious symbols is always society itself. Likewise, I find it possible to appropriate his views on the social functions of ritual without thereby reducing the meaning of ritual simply to its social or psychological functions. For Durkheim's views, see *The Elementary Forms of the Religious Life*, trans. Joseph Ward Swain (New York: Macmillan Company, 1915); cf. Harry Alpert, "Durkheim's Functional Theory of Ritual," in Robert A. Nisbet, *Emile Durkheim* (Englewood Cliffs, N.J.: Prentice-Hall, 1965), pp. 137–41; and Steven Lukes, *Emile Durkheim: His Life and Work* (London: Allen Lane, 1973), pp. 470–74.

ened. The meaning arc which begins in acts of individual interpretation and projection is made dense by meanings that are
evoked in the experience of many individuals by shared types
and symbols. What emerges is the full richness and variety of
social worlds, one part of which is a complex and textured value
sensibility. When such a value sensibility reflects the presence of
a deeply shared value paradigm, then individual interpretation
and projection is dialectically related to images of social identity
and destiny.

It is also within the moral community that there arises the
possibility that moral discourse and discernment will render the
experience of individuals problematic and will actually induce
social change. At such points, human beings do not cease to interpret and project; rather, they seek to achieve an interpretation of what is going on and projects adequate to that interpretation. Likewise, human beings will not cease to behave in a
ritual manner, but rather will seek to embody their emerging
typical and symbolic grasp of experience in vital forms which
are expressive of the new meaning horizons being evoked in
their experience through social change.

The moral agent in the social world has been portrayed as intending the world in the light of a horizon of value meaning
which is coexperienced in a moral community. The general
possibilities that ground experiences of value and moral experience indicate that such realities are an essential part of the
human being and the human world. The experience of value
qualifies determinate human action in various ways, according
to the nature of the value paradigm and according to the way it
is accented in relation to other possible experiences. A center of
value there must be because the human being is a valuing
creature and the human social world is value-laden; but that
value center and the concrete relations it recommends will vary
greatly among groups and across social time.

This conclusion brings us back to a concern with which we
began, namely, the pluralism of the modern world and of contemporary experience. If anything, the analysis in these pages
has deepened this problem by affirming it and by showing the
grounds in human agency upon which it rests. Does this mean

that no paradigms of value meaning are better than any others? Or is moral experience and the values that evoke it hopelessly bound up with the relativities of space, time, and individual idiosyncracy? An answer to this question would, of course, require another type of analysis. Given the tendencies of this argument, such a treatment would take seriously paradigms of value meaning that affirm and support the existence and well-being of others rather than value persuasions that lead to the oppression or destruction of others. Such a value center would clearly be humanistic; but there is nothing in the foregoing analysis that would prevent it from becoming associated with meanings evoked by the luminous symbols of a concrete religious tradition.

Conclusion

It is time to look back over the entire argument in order to assess what appear to be the major contributions this analysis has made to the task of constructive ethical reflection. One contribution is methodological, whereas the others are more substantive and theoretical in character.

The methodological contribution may be treated briefly. The argument should have demonstrated the gains that are possible at the descriptive level when the phenomenological perspective is applied to moral life and experience. This contribution is viewed as supplemental to other perspectives and procedures that are available to ethicists in their work. For example, philosophical themes, linguistic analysis, sociological perspectives, and theological base points will continue as important sources for ethical construction and will not immediately be displaced by phenomenological description. What has been demonstrated, however, is that phenomenological description can achieve some tasks that are not possible given the limitation of the concepts and methods of other perspectives.

The methodological contribution is related to certain basic theoretical notions that have become apparent in the course of the analysis. Five of these substantive contributions deserve to be emphasized in order to be clear about what was attempted in the argument and what was accomplished.

First, Chapter I proposed a theory of the agent which grounds the entire analysis. Central to this view is the notion of intentional consciousness, an interpretation that stands in a clearly identifiable philosophical tradition. This view of human consciousness represents a theoretical commitment which is necessary to the understanding of moral agency developed later in the analysis. This perspective upon conscious experience is not simply employed heuristically but in fact entails at least minimal claims to greater adequacy than other interpretations. For example, an epistemological implication of this perspective is that acts of knowing are neither a consequence of the conformity of the mind to some objective order nor merely a consequence of subjective projection. The primordial dialectic between subject and object is held as central and as more adequate to describe how the reality of our conscious lives actually appears.

Second, the view of the conscious agent as a center from which meaning emerges became the ground for developing an understanding of the nature of value. Values are meanings intended by conscious agents and are intersubjectively shared in the social world. Again, this view rejects the tendency to understand values as objective essences, or at least as realities that are radically outside the human world and human experience. Also rejected is the view that renders values simply as projections of individual needs or feelings, and thus as ephemeral and untrustworthy aspects of human experience. As shared meaning structures, values have a certain objectivity, especially when they appear in the form of paradigms that qualify entire cultures or epochs. And values have an inescapable subjective root in that they depend for their experiential reality upon the continual fiat of the agent, granting them the accent of reality. But the dialectical character of the experience of value becomes the most adequate explanatory perspective for this analysis. The objectivity of values is more fragile than most objectivists would maintain; and values are more durable than would appear from the position that most subjectivists adopt.

Third, the view of the social world as constituted in experience by types and symbols enabled us to grasp dimensions of richness and complexity that other perspectives ignore. It was within this analysis that the basic theory of the pairing capacity of consciousness was utilized to show how various sorts of human transcendence were rendered possible. The analysis made clear how typifying consciousness constituted a world in a basic sense and also enabled us to bring that world within reach. In addition to this form of transcendence, there is also the transcendence rendered possible by complex symbols that span more than one meaning horizon. It was in the view of symbol, and especially in the understanding of art, religion, and morality, that we glimpsed some of the most impressive manifestations of human transcendence. Indeed, the argument at this point drove toward the border of questions concerning the source of symbolic capacities, a series of issues that would require a different sort of analysis to address.

Fourth, the entire statement moved toward an affirmation of the reality of moral experience, despite the fragmentation and pluralism of modern life. The effect of phenomenological description was to unearth a human consciousness rich with possibility and capable of migrations which, perhaps in our time, are too confined by a scientific worldview. Despite this, the argument was clear at the point that fantasy, imagination, memory, and other elements which form the conditions of possibility for moral agency may not be reduced to the status of dependent and diminished realities in the light of a series of scientific objectifications—even if these objectifications are fashioned by professional ethicists.

The reality sense of the experience of value, as is the case for religious and aesthetic sensibilities, arises as a consequence of features that are essential and not accidental to the human being and the human social world. The object of ethical reflection, namely the moral life and moral experience in its subjective and intersubjective forms, is a persistent datum which will not disappear in the pure light of what may be conceived to be a paradigm of meaning that is more adequate and real. The experience of value has its own relative autonomy and is a form of human transcendence that is universal.

Fifth, the analysis aimed at exposing some of the roots of ordinary moral experience. For the most part, this level of experience is routinized and beyond the scope of our attention. And yet it is within ordinary life that some of the most monumental experiences of transcendence occur. It is within the taken-for-granted dimensions of experience that face-to-face interaction constitutes the substance of the social world. And it is within this social world that paradigms of value meaning arise, enabling moral experience to become widely shared and deeply influential in the way human knowing and doing occur.

This archaeology of the moral agent in the social world has pointed toward questions of religious and aesthetic meaning. These forms of transcendence, along with the experience of value, point beyond themselves to sources that would require another sort of analysis to explore. The final word here should be that approaching the experiences of value, religion, and art "from below," in terms of their anthropological grounds, neither affirms nor denies the task that would be involved in proposing an argument about the broader referential significance of these primordial and persistent human realities.

Index